HOW TO MAKE
A BETTER PROFIT
IN THE LAW OFFICE
... Year After Year

.... Featuring the MMM* Principle

BY
BERTRAM S. SILVER

*Make More Money

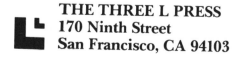

THE THREE L PRESS
170 Ninth Street
San Francisco, CA 94103

The author accepts no responsibility for the legality of any forms or ideas presented, as laws and interpretations differ in various states. They are furnished for information, ideas and indication of what the author has done.

Bertram S. Silver

First Printing September 1978
Second Printing October 1979

Library of Congress Catalog Card No. 78-69730
ISBN-0-9601938-1-2

Dedication

To My Three "Wives,"
Barbara, Mertie, and Marty

TABLE OF CONTENTS

Foreword   viii

Prologue   ix

I. THE LAW OFFICE, or
    It's Also A Business   1

II. THE TYPICAL LAWYER, or
    His Affairs Are In An Absolute Mess   5

III. IS THERE ETHICS IN LAW? or
    Be Honest With Yourself   11

IV. HOW LARGE A FIRM, or
    Big Is Not Necessarily Better   15

V. HOW TO FIND A PARTNER, or
    *A Second Wife Is Almost As Important
    As The First*   21

VI. HOW TO LOOK FOR AN ASSOCIATE, or
    *It Doesn't Mean You Must Be Of
    The Same Mold*   29

VII. HOW TO LOOK FOR A SECRETARY, or
    *They'll Run The Office Anyway,
    So Find Capable Ones*   33

VIII. THE PROCEDURE MANUAL, or
    Don't Confuse Me With Facts   41

IX. FEES AND COSTS, or
    Do Lawyers Always Overcharge?   47

X. IS SPEED ESSENTIAL IN ALL CASES?, or
    Only If You Want A Greater Profit   59

XI. CORPORATE OR PARTNERSHIP, or
    There Really Is No Choice   67

XII. PENSION AND PROFIT SHARING PLANS,
    or , *We Never Missed A Beat*   75

XIII. KEEPING RECORDS LIKE A BUSINESS, or
   Why Not? It Is One! 85

XIV. THE "PERSONAL" CLIENT-LAWYER
   RELATIONSHIP, or
   Switching Cases And Clients Is Good For All ... 91

XV. THE ORGANIZED FIRM, or
   Meetings And Statistics Only Confuse Me 97

XVI. OBTAINING NEW CLIENTS, or
   Now You Can Advertise 103

XVII. ECONOMY AND EFFICIENCY, or
   It's Worth A Try To Save Money 109

XVIII. A HAPPY OFFICE PAYS DIVIDENDS, or
   It Takes More Than Just Tickling 115

XIX. CONTINUING LAW EDUCATION, or
   At Fifty I Can Still Learn–But Will I? 119

XX. VACATION AND SABBATICALS, or
   Your Ego Gets Bruised When
   They Don't Miss You 125

   EPILOGUE 130

FOREWORD

My partner, Bert Silver, is an original. Only he could have written this unique, practical, useable book about a successful law practice. As a whole person, he offers many insights about the law practice in relation to the living experience. A mere technician he is not; but he appreciates the values of precision, planning and implementation. These "keys" to success have worked for him, for us and most importantly, for our public clients.

Unlike some law firms, we have no retainers. No one need come to us for service. Any client can terminate his relationship with us instantly and without notice. Therefore, we are forced to operate in the present and for the future. Yesterday's achievements do not suffice. Thus, the emphasis on systems, controls, planning and such innovations as sabbaticals for stress-living lawyers.

This is a condensed volume, one that is loaded with specific, invaluable suggestions. Bert Silver did not conceive each of them but he has put them all together and we have lived by them unusually well. We suggest that this book be re-read more than once so that some of the subtleties will be revealed. If read and applied, you, your family and your clients will be rewarded as we have.

MARTIN J. ROSEN

PROLOGUE

This book will make you more money. If you read this book from a positive view with an attitude of willingness to accept, you will gain constructive ideas which will increase your take-home dollars.

This is a simply written book, so don't be lulled into a sense of simplicity and shrug it off. It will accomplish more for your profits than any one major case you've ever handled.

I've never been able to find one simple book for lawyers, like myself, describing down-to-earth practices and procedures which makes a lawyer WANT to be more efficient and profitable.* Further, mature lawyers generally won't recognize that their management of the law office is faulty and less profitable than it should be. This book was written to fill the need for a lawyer's business and profit manual and to make him WANT to follow it.

---

*There are hundreds of good articles and books on the separate subjects of forms, layout, partnership vs. corporation, specialization, and other subjects. There are also books of advice for young lawyers on particular office subjects and fields, and even volumes on starting law practices.

Reading a lawyer's business manual is about as exciting as watching paint dry. This book will keep you interested while showing you:

1. How you can bring you or your law firm more profit and free time without basically altering your style or capabilities.

2. That most lawyers are minimizing their profits; this book will help you maximize such profits.

3. How maximizing profits will allow a better quality of service to the client—the public.

How To Make A Better Profit In The Law Office—Year After Year is a positive book of actual practices and procedures adopted to maximize profits and income and, at the same time, improve the service to the client.

It is NOT a form book, nor does it recommend any set forms for use. Other books and services most adequately detail suggestions for time sheets, procedure manual contents, billings, vouchers, filing and the myriad of other forms. This book will demonstrate the *need* for some form and system, but not a particular one.

Nor does this book go into detail on the methods discussed. For example, I write of a young partner buying into the firm, but while there are several methods of evaluating the cost and many systems for payment, I don't try to go into those phases. I discuss the *need* for buy-sell agreements, but the innumerable ways to handle the valuations, methods and payouts are not included here. To try to include suggestions on all such matters would make this manual too cumbersome.

Many, or most, lawyers are used to giving advice, but they seldom consider taking the same advice themselves even though it increases their efficiency and profitability. Most are simply too hide-bound to change style. Call it ego, perhaps. In an excusatory manner they will say to us:

"You have Marty Rosen as a partner. . . ."

"You have Bert Silver as a partner. . . ."

"You're specialized so it'll work for you, 'but not for me.'"

"Your practice is different than ours."

"You have a different class of clientele."

"You have different kinds of partners than I."

"Our area has a tougher competitive position than yours."

The proof is that the methods and systems we've adopted, cribbed, adapted and instituted have worked not only for us but for other lawyers, who, after listening to me on my soap box, have adopted a few or many of these methods and systems. The beneficiaries are working no more hours, usually far less, and are more effective and efficient while making more money.

There are three basic methods of adding to your profit in a law office. Each is covered here:

(1) *Tax Savings Opportunities,* such as profit sharing and pension plans, incorporating, and separate fiscal years.

(2) *Economizing* through cutting present expenses, without lessening the ability to produce.

(3) *Efficiencies* which allow more time to practice law at the hourly rate you're billing.

We use corporate form, Profit Sharing and Pension Plans, Sabbaticals, vacations, interchanging of clients (even on on-going cases), joint billing, expedition of cases and many other money-making systems. Most of these methods are profitable and adaptable to all firms. At first I was going to except the larger firms of 50 or so lawyers. It seemed that such size presupposed high organizational standards and use of money-making systems; then I looked at them closely. Most large firms are a group of specialized smaller firms joined together. I found rivalries, resisting forces and a lack of many of the systems discussed here; they can well use some of the ideas set forth in this book.

I'm afraid, however, that most lawyers won't take advantage of the ideas that will make them money! They counsel their clients to adopt efficient systems, but most lawyers are traditionalists, conservative, hesitant, too busy or too lazy to adopt their own. They go on and on with smaller profitability and longer hours than they should. Malpractice against themselves!

Many reading this volume will swear that some of the ideas are obvious. The reader may shrug them off, claiming he already follows THAT rule, but, be honest with yourself!

Don't rationalize by saying that it's too hard or too late to change. As my esteemed partner has continually remarked when we institute each innovation, "We haven't missed a beat!"

Also, remember that with the exception of the Profit Sharing and Pension Plans, no one action, system or procedure will make or save you a very large amount of money, but adoption of many will measurably do so. Try it—you will be surprised . . .

We can never overlook our high professional duty to the client and the public which is the primary responsibility of a lawyer. The innovation and use of systems and processes that allow far greater profitability per lawyer and efficiency within the office can never be instituted if they result in lowered standards or inferior work. You'll find, however, that these innovations result in improved standards and faster high quality work. We'll stack our reputation, achievements, high standards, and expedited service to the client and public against any law firm.

Note: With apologies to my daughter Lani, for ease of writing I'll refer to lawyers as "he" rather than continually saying "he or she." Male chauvinist?! Probably, although we've hired two women lawyers in our small office. Also, when I refer to a partner, I'm also referring to a shareholder, if the firm is incorporated; and when I speak of partnership, I'll also mean professional corporation, unless otherwise specified.

I

THE LAW OFFICE

or

It's Also A Business

"Time is the lawyer's capital.

Every lawyer has just so many more years in which to practice law. Every day, ever hour, he has that much less capital—not a pleasant thought, but it cannot be escaped. It might as well be faced, and an effort made to do something about it.

To make the most of his constantly diminishing capital, a lawyer must make the most of every hour and every minute. One effective step in this direction is to make his law office as efficient as possible—to organize his staff to work for him, whether his staff consists of one part-time stenographer, or of a whole group of lawyers and secretaries. . . .

A lawyer cannot afford to do, himself, anything that he can hire a girl to do. This extends to many things in addition to bookkeeping, indexing files, and keeping time records, and is a basic fundamental."

"A Law Office System" by Arch M. Antrall
The Practical Lawyers Law Office Manual, No. 1, pg. 1*

Of course law is a "calling." We have the highest duty of professional conduct and an obligation to accomplish our client's objective in the most professional manner. Of course we are charged with an ethical standard higher than any lay business; and, of course, we should perform public service that brings more stature to the profession.

All true and accepted, but is there any reason that all of these tenets cannot be achieved and abided by, and still increase an office's profitability? The practice of law is a profession, but secondarily it is a business. If you can take home $60,000 a year instead of $40,000, accomplish the same result, and not charge the client any more, you have given your family a $20,000 per year higher standard of living. If in doing it you can work less time you spend more leisure time with your family (or at tennis or golf). If you don't take this double opportunity, you're wrong.

Let's equate it another way. If a lawyer spends five hours a month innovating and following good business ideas he might gross $1,000 more per month—that's $200 per hour. In effect, he's hired himself out at $200 per hour for this work, more by far than the clients are usually paying him. But many lawyers practice in firms. The aggregate of five hours a month needed to adopt the business-like practices suggested here, increase *each* lawyer's efficiency, output and gross billing; thus, there is a multiplying effect.

It's my educated estimate* that a busy firm of 4–6 lawyers can increase their gross income by an average of $10,000 per month with only a small (or no) increase in expenses. Larger firms should be able proportionately, to accomplish more.

These have to be startling figures to those of you who feel overworked (and in most cases, underpaid). Without any

---

*My partners say I'm uncanny in the accuracy of my projections.

loss of quality you can make more money if you're willing to modify traditional, hide-bound, antiquated methods and procedures.

The same innovations and systems and philosophies will be applicable whether your firm consists of general practitioners, tort, corporate, patent or other specialists. The adoption of an efficient business-like approach to your professional practice has proven to be profitable.

No matter what your age or specialty, whether you practice alone or with partners, whether in a partnership or corporation, please read the pages that follow with an open mind. If you do that and adopt even some of the ideas that you don't now practice I can virtually guarantee that this book will increase your profits considerably without in any way impairing your ethics or professional commitment.

The really overworked lawyer may be making $100,000 per year, but if he's putting in 12 hours a day plus Saturdays and/or Sundays, he's really only earning $50,000–60,000 per year, but he's doing double work. In our office we make good income but attempt assiduously to avoid working Saturdays, Sundays or nights. The thoughts in this book, if followed, will help you to limit your hours *and* make you more money. Try it, your family will like it.

Before I start to tell you *what to do* to make your firm more profitable and efficient you're entitled to know my credentials.

I've been a practicing lawyer for 30 years, first in a general practice and then in a specialized field; I am considered by others as eminently successful in every phase of practice—that includes ethics, professional achievements, money making and business.* I'm a past president of our

---

*But perhaps not modesty.

national specialized bar association, and founding senior partner of what is considered to be a prestigious and respected firm in our field. I seem to have an affinity for business, making money and innovating organizational efficiencies. We have by comparison, the most profitable (per lawyer) and most business-like office of all those with whom we have come in contact. Because of my propensities in this area, I've been asked to be a consultant to other law firms, to adopt for them similar systems and procedures to that which we've done for ourselves. I've eased out of the day-to-day law practice with money I've earned solely from the practice.

Now let's see how profitability can be accomplished for you.

Now let's see if you want it done for you.

RULE:

Time spent on planning and putting business practices in effect will pay substantially more money to you.

II

THE TYPICAL LAWYER

or

His Affairs Are In An Absolute Mess

The good lawyer demands his clients have business-like procedures and safeguards. He counsels his clients on having future planning and foresight. He reminds them of their need for a will or an update of the old one, keeping the corporate records in order, sound financial stability, safeguards against adverse results from untimely death, proper insurance of many kinds, memos and notes on underlying facts pertaining to a suit, domestic financial settlements on divorce or remarriage, and a myriad of protections depending on the circumstances and business.

Does the lawyer do this for himself and his firm? In most cases NO! The lawyer can give advice, but seldom does he take it.

A large percentage of the lawyers that I've talked to have never drawn a will, or if they have, it was years ago and it's badly outdated. We all act like we are immortal and it's only the other person who will die at some time in the unknown future. The good lawyer encourages his clients to prepare and execute a will, but he doesn't translate that need to himself. Instead, he does exactly what his client has been doing, but he doesn't have a lawyer to push him.

The same testamentary rules apply to you as to your clients. Your estate will be stuck with a bond; your wife may live in privation because she has to share assets with your children who don't need them or will squander them. Worse, she may have a double tax problem because while you carefully preserved marital deductions for your clients and their spouse, you didn't do it for yourself.

You counsel clients to keep a fairly up-to-date list of assets (and their location) including all bank accounts, stocks, insurance policies and the like. Why? So on death the widow, and you, the lawyer, can readily find them; they won't be lost forever. But you probably don't do it for yourself, your spouse or the person who will help probate your estate. Seldom, if ever, do you or your firm draw an honest up-to-date balance sheet.

Most small firms have no Buy-Sell Agreement or Survivorship Purchase Agreement—it's left in a half lit *nether* world. You feel your practice is different than a business; you and your partners joined together haphazardly because you wanted to practice together; the practice wasn't worth much to start so what's the need for all of this paper work? You forget completely that while it had little marketable value at the inception when you were young, you've built into it a value of repeated satisfied clients; a phone number, files, a name, an ongoing goodwill entity. If your partner dies first, you the survivor, will get a big windfall without paying proper value if there's no Survivorship Purchase Agreement. The reverse is true if you die first. Assume that you want to practice law elsewhere and leave the now flourishing 6-man firm you started, if there is no Buy-Sell Agreement, you may find that you leave without the phone number, clients' files, books, client's phone numbers and maybe even your desk. The pittance in money you may get from the firm, if any, can only be increased by a time consuming, expensive, bitter law suit. All of this can be avoided by doing for yourself what you counsel your clients to do.

Where a corporate form of practice is used, 8 out of 11 lawyers I asked, candidly admitted that their corporate minutes and records are not current. Five of these eight firms also acknowledged that they keep their clients' corporate minutes and filings to date and have a follow-up system for this task. Their own corporation isn't included and so its work doesn't get done even routinely.

A lawyer friend of mine believes his business clients should have an on-going practice of job evaluation and salary review periodically, but when I asked him if they did this in his office for their secretaries, receptionist and associates, he smiled and admitted they did not. When I persisted and asked if they did it for the partners, he was aghast. Yet, why not?

Compounding the non-business-like practice of lawyers is their habit of procrastination. Since the client isn't on our carpet every day demanding that his matter move we tend to procrastinate. We're busy so we put off that which we can. This same habit is carried over to our own affairs. It gets to be a habit and frankly, as we shall see, it's an unnecessarily costly one to the lawyer and the client.

It takes many lawyers 6–12 months to draw a will; divorces drag while one lawyer "tries to get hold of the other lawyer"; law suits are 2–4 years in progress. Is it any wonder that our bookkeeper after two and one-half years of personal legal machination* stated that the logo for lawyers should be a *snail*.

The constant postponement of drawing the complaint, filing it, stipulations, pleadings, briefs, motions, agreed orders, interrogatories, answers, settlement conferences, the trial itself, and all other phases have become interminable and embarrassing. I checked twenty-five files (in our County Clerk's office) of cases ready to go to trial. The delays from the above type postponements were horrendous and constituted almost as much paper work as the substantive case itself. The cost is high, even forgetting about the lost time—which is a cost itself. In talking to lawyers who are participants in these delays, I questioned them as to who pays for the lost time involved in the telephone calls, orders, and filings that lead up to the agreement to delay. It became apparent that some of the cost is borne by the client but much of it by the lawyer who is the cause of it. If it's a fixed or contingent fee case, then all this time is a loss to you, the lawyer who absorbs it. If you don't procrastinate and delay, your clients' charge could be lower or your profits higher. You would make money by not having to eat the time you now waste. You've made money and time for yourself to do other things.

Most lawyers are bad businessmen. It's easy for me to say to all of you:

- Draw a will

- Have a Buy-Sell Agreement

- Have a Survivorship Purchase Agreement

- Have a Financial Statement

- Keep your own corporate records to date

- DON'T PROCRASTINATE

---

*Fortunately, not using our firm.

If you don't start thinking like a businessman as well as a lawyer, you won't change your slovenly habits. This book will make you realize that your are losing money from procrastination; that with better habits *and no more work* that money would go in your pocket. Your family is courting pain and disaster when you die without a will or Survivorship Purchase Agreement, or when you break up your firm and have no Buy-Sell Agreement, or when the IRS comes in and disregards your corporate entity because you forgot to keep corporate records.

The irreconcileable part of this is that DOING these things would save you money, not cost you any.

RULES:

1. Put your own business affairs in order exactly as if you were a client.

2. Don't procrastinate.

III
IS THERE ETHICS IN LAW?
or
Be Honest With Yourself

In this chapter let's talk of an intangible philosophy, then from here we'll go on to more concrete specifics.

With a few exceptions, the personal friendships developed between lawyer and client are transitory. It may be a business relationship only. If you think it's more than a "what have you done for me lately" syndrome, see what happens if you lose a few cases, or aggravate your "friend" by an overcharge, a poor result or an unpleasant incident. If you die they probably, after brief clucking of the tongue, will quickly wonder aloud as to which other lawyer or firm will break their neck for them as you did for so many years.

What am I leading up to? Simply that the client may sell you down the river if it will mean an appreciable advantage to him. He'll attempt to make *you* (not him) fudge and skirt the line of propriety to benefit him; he'll expect *you* to take advantage of the opposition, even if it's a questionable tactic, but it's not his license or certificate on the line. If you're disbarred or censured he's not going to support you or your family.

So . . . play square in every phase of your activity. It will all pay off in the long pull.

Play square with all of the lawyers you will deal with. Keep your word in every case and give them the courtesy break similar to that which you'd want and someday need. If you promise to produce a witness, produce him, don't "sincerely" pretend excuses. If you promise work product by a certain date, make sure it's there. If you promise not to dispute a request for extension of time, don't protest it. I dealt with two particular lawyers in thirty years who absolutely could not be trusted to keep their word. The result was that any request of theirs, any promise they made or any representation *had to be in writing.* We understand that several commissioners and judges made the same demand of them; this did not help their clients.

The temptation of money is great. That's why the Canon of Ethics and Bar Rules so carefully require separation of money into OURS versus THEIRS. Follow it carefully. Keep your trust accounts absolutely separate; make sure the client knows it's separate, and he'll respect you for it and won't mind making advances. Make sure probate money, if you have any, is likewise set aside and available for the use intended.

If you handle down payments for sales which you put in your trust account, don't release it to your client if a dispute later arises and you think he's right. Hold it until the matter is settled; by taking it you've either expressly or impliedly promised the other side that you'd do so. The client won't or may not be able to pay it back to you later if you're ordered to release the down payment to the other side.

The promises you make should be kept regardless of who they are made to. If you employ a new secretary and vaguely promise her a $50 raise in three months "if she works out," don't forget it or assuage your guilt over not keeping the promise by rationalizing that she's not as good as she represented. Either talk to her, pay her or let her go. Don't welch or weasel.

We're not trying to be Boy Scouts, but keeping the promises you make and playing fair with other lawyers, clients and your office personnel will be the first step to long range profits because these people will trust you and depend on your work and all of your actions. It raises your stature and brings more business.

RULES:

1. Be 100% ethical and absolutely above board with the clients, lawyers, and office staff.

2. Keep your promises.

IV
HOW LARGE A FIRM
or
Big Is Not Necessarily Better

Any lawyer who practices without a partner is simply not interested in maximizing profits and efficiencies and an easier overall life. A strong statement? No, just a fact. The loner pays a very, very high price for his ego, total independence and the right to "do it my way."

> *"First, let us ask, why* any *firm? Why not a bar composed entirely of lone practitioners? A wise, old judge once explained his earliest partnership with another young lawyer (no associates). "I liked office work," he said, "and Charlie liked to try cases. So it seemed wise to share expenses. As to dividing fees, you know, any fool can fry a fish, but it takes an artist to catch one. . . ."*

> *However large or small the firm, we may surmise that the principles stated in this homely reasoning are among the factors which lead to law partnerships:*

> • *Different lawyers prefer different types of work.*

> • *Some lawyers excel as workmen, others at attracting clients.*

> • *Sharing the expense of lay employees, rent, library, telephone, etc., is an economy for lawyer and client."*
>
> "Some Comments on Large Law Firms"
> by Edwin C. Austin
> *The Practical Lawyer's Law Office Manual,*
> No. 2, pgs. 66–67.*

You can add to that several other salient factors:

- Several lawyers in a firm mean more vacation; without in any way jeopardizing a client's pressing work while one is playing. Even sabbaticals are possible.†

- Several lawyers make it economically feasible to institute a qualified Profit Sharing Plan and Pension Plan which is the best tax shelter most lawyers can ever hope to get. As a corollary, it also makes the corporate use more feasible which has other benefits.

- The joinder of more than two lawyers makes it economically feasible to have workable systems and record keeping that of themselves save more money for each lawyer.

- The joint views of different minds produce better tactics if periodic discussions of cases between them is the rule.

Not only does the lawyer get tangible and economic benefit from a legal association or partnership but the client whom he has sworn to help, gets improved and more assured services.

---

*Copyright 1956 by The American Law Institute. Reprinted with the permission of The American Law Institute-American Bar Association Committee on Continuing Professional Education.

†I hadn't intended to bring that subject up so early. I was trying to break you in slowly.

If you have a firm of lawyers (two or more) the important question arises—How Big Should it Grow?

As noted earlier, most lawyers are lousy businessmen. Even the size of the firm is never planned but grows and wanes in a haphazard fashion. The standard method of most growing firms is to increase their size as they obtain more business then the present members can handle, and then they take in more business to keep the new members busy, and then ... BUT there never is an analysis, let alone an *upgrading* of their present clientele by evaluating:

- the type of work being taken in

- the profitability of various phases of the present work

- the desirability of retaining some of the present clients

Yes, I said UPGRADING. It's a smart, ethical and profitable legal practice. The small client who started with you, as a young lawyer, who chiseled fees and took too much of your time may have grown with you, but if he still chisels fees, doesn't pay, constantly complains and takes more time than you're billing him for, he would be better off sent to a young outside lawyer who needs the business to start. Don't talk to me of "long friendship" and joint sentiment. Watch when his long-time doctor dies and he doesn't even go to the funeral.

At one stage we found that 17% of our time was spent on a particular type of work that brought in only 8% of our revenue. By declining that type of work we were able to devote more time to better paying work. We upgraded. Several years later we found that four clients in particular were taking 12% of our time, but for historical reasons were only being billed 7½% of our revenue. Subjectively, we also knew that they gave us more trouble than most other clients. We slowly sent them elsewhere to other lawyers who wanted their work. That's also upgrading.

I can tell you now that most lawyers probably will not have the guts to upgrade their practices. Upgrading means analyzing your practice and the profitability of its component parts. If you find that three constantly troublesome clients are taking 20% of your annual time but paying 10% of your gross revenue, get rid of them instead of hiring another associate. If you don't replace them you can take that time for clients who are carrying their own weight. If a client is constantly delinquent in your statement, 6-12 months or more, ask your accountant to figure how much discount you're giving by not charging him a monthly service charge. You can be sure he's currently paying other bills, particularly when the creditors dun him. The point is if he won't keep fairly current and you've warned, pleaded and cajoled him, then drop him and give better service to the guy who pays promptly. It's called upgrading.

Assuming you have upgraded and by logical pre-thought have expanded the firm, the question then arises as to how big it should ultimately become. Of course, there are firms from 2 to 500 lawyers. It makes no difference how big the firm is as long as it's done on a pre-thought, systematic basis with cogent reasons and with profitable expectancy, but some firms of 200 lawyers are as disorganized and poor in profitability as some with 2 or 3 lawyers.

In our case, I made a study years ago and found that in our field about four lawyers was the best number for optimum results in client service, firm profitability, time off and ease of administration. Beyond that the profits of the seniors grew very little (15% gross pre-tax for the seniors) and didn't compensate for the added administration, space, supervision and communication problems that resulted. So we have an inviolate rule of a maximum of *five* lawyers.

Why five when four is optimum? Because we had also decided on:

- one month's vacation (with pay) for each lawyer.
- a six-month sabbatical* (with pay) each 5 years.

With five on the team, four were always present. It works. We even went so far as to have only five lawyers' offices built into our new suite so that we would not be tempted to get bigger—just to be getting bigger. The point is that it was done analytically and methodically; it didn't just happen.

I'm not saying five lawyers is the correct size for *your* firm—or any other firm. I am saying that to simply continue to grow larger to take in more clients and then to take in more clients to get larger defies reason. Give serious thought to the personal economics of the size of the firm and how large you should really grow. How will the continued increase affect your time and income? Look ahead—as a good businessman would—and see whether the added costs of more space, moving and overhead, together with your added time and supervision warrant the growth. Maybe it's only your ego that's pushing for an increase in firm size.

RULES:

1. Practice with more than one lawyer.

2. Upgrade your business by getting rid of the marginal clients.

3. Limit the size of your firm on a pre-planned basis.

---

*I said that dirty word again. See Chapter XX. (When you come to it.)

V
HOW TO FIND A PARTNER
or
A Second Wife Is Almost As Important As The First

I've already pointed out that practicing alone is costly and foolish. Partnership* has so many advantages.

The choosing of partners is a major decision often made lightly or even accidentally. The results of these decisions are monumental in terms of money, time, investment and long-term consequences. Of course, partnerships can be formed experimentally; but the effort and expense to put two or more partners together is costly and once together there is a lack of reluctance to split. Many stay together from lack of inertia even if it's not a good union. Just the hiring of an associate, while less permanent, is a considerable investment when you count your time and effort to train the younger lawyer in your ways. There is strong reason in both cases to plan ahead in making a choice.

---

*Again, when I refer to "Partnership", I mean it in the sense of several lawyers together; it could be as a legal partnership, professional corporation or association.

What are the criteria to be aware of? They may vary in degree depending upon whether:

- two older lawyers are talking of joining forces

- a firm is taking in a young lawyer as a partner

- a firm is taking in a young lawyer as an associate

Regardless of which situation you are faced with at that moment, there are certain similar criteria that must be considered.

First and foremost, the partners must have a genuine liking and respect for each other. It's a long-time marriage. I know there are some successful partnerships where the partners are personally incompatible, but these are exceptions. Why add the possibility of constant aggravation to our daily practice?

On a personal basis, let me say my longest term partner and I have been very fortunate in really liking and respecting one another.* Both of us being strong personalities we've taken an interesting position to maintain our relationship. If I don't feel strongly about a matter, we can do it his way. He feels the same. In all our years I've felt strongly about a matter twice, he once. The other acceded with no question. We like and admire each other; this helps.

Next, it's important to know whether the long range objectives of the future partners are compatible. Just because you respect each other's style or enjoy drinking together or talking law together, it is not reason to practice in tandem. Explore the other's long-range preferences of the type and style of practice. Do you both want to concentrate on similar fields? If you have completely different interests, a partnership would save money be sharing expenses, *but* the other

---

*The same liking and respect is present with the younger partners also; it just hasn't existed as long.

benefits are not present; it's like having different law firms sharing the same office.

Other mutual objectives should be explored. Does each partner want substantial time off in the coming years or is one a workaholic? If that's the situation, resentment and anger will result if there is a disparity of time worked by each of them.

Do both partners want to avoid work on Saturday, Sunday or nights, except when on trial or an absolute emergency?

Is money important to each, so that they have mutual long range goals? If one is wealthy and practicing "for the fun of it" while the other needs to make money, there may be a problem. So similar financial objectives are important.

Strangely, it's not necessary that both be businesslike and administratively inclined as long as: (a) one partner is, and (b) the others accept the fact that for the benefit of all the practice must be run as a business.

It's also not necessary that the legal style of each member be the same. It's probably advantageous to have different styles in the same office. We don't try to make our associates or younger partners conform to our substantive style of research, writing, or pleadings. We feel that each of us is capable and qualified and each grew with his own idiosyncratic methods peculiar to himself. But note, I said we don't try to change their *substantive style*. We do believe in a consistent mode of form in the typing of letters, briefs, pleadings, contracts and other documents. The reason for this uniformity will be explained later in this book. We also believe that if one of our systems of abstracting, research, memorandum or pleading is notably better and less time consuming than one used by our partners' or associates', we'll expose him to it and discuss the matter; so hopefully, he'll even substantively alter his style. Overall we leave him the professional license to substantively practice in the manner he is most comfortable with and which produces the best results.

What else do we look for in a partner? A lawyer with much ego and confidence in himself, but who will subordinate these for the betterment of the firm, i.e., he won't be hurt when his view doesn't prevail in every discussion. As a corollary, he will accept the fact that *he's dispensible to the client but not to the firm.* Why? Because we exchange and transfer cases (more of this later), so we can: (a) give the client better service, and (b) take more time off without delaying clients' pending cases. Our ego isn't bruised when we realize someone else is handling a matter and a client in a comparable workmanlike manner. We aren't afraid to go on a one month (or 6 month) vacation for fear that those left behind will find we're not indispensible. We concede we're not indispensible to the client, but by joining forces cooperatively we are each an integral part of a team that works for each other at maximum profitability. For that we each give up some ego!

In deciding upon a new partner we look at whether as an associate, he worked more closely with his other associates and seniors than his secretary. We've found that many budding lawyers and incipient partners try to compartmentalize their efforts so that what they do accomplish is more immediately apparent to others. It's empire building! We want the lawyers to cooperate and work together with no overt emphasis on a particular secretary. We do not want him to play politics in the personal office problems of his secretary. The firm comes first and the lawyers will be with the firm the longest.

Incidentally, when we pick a partner we give him every chance to succeed and lean over in his favor, but once we know he's the wrong one for us, we terminate, then and there. We don't try to torture a bad partner and nice guy into a good partner. We're interested in a long-range situation for both sides; if he's not to be permanent, then sever the relationship quickly.

I'd also suggest you stop the usual reluctance to expeditiously bring in a young associate because "I had to work 8 years to own a piece of the action and so must you." If after 2 or 3 or 4 years you decide that the associate is a gem and you want him with you, start bringing him in right then. It helps his stature and ego and helps you by having a "partner" deal with the client instead of an associate. Also important, he probably will not be tempted to leave.

Assuming you have properly set up your firm and picked the right associate, how do you bring him into the firm as a partner?

Originally, we let them buy in; they either bought shares or a partnership interest right then. Sure, they could pay for it on time but they owned a piece of the action. We found, however, in two cases the new partners found private practice responsibilities as a member of a firm not to their liking and one went into private industry, while another went to teaching. While one gave us no trouble at all, the other made demands far in excess of those we had made of him when he came in. On several issues there was a feeling of distaste and unpleasantness.

Thereafter we instituted a two-step system. For two years the young lawyer is made a "profit sharing"* partner. He's given the same percentage share of profits as he'd normally have bought in for; he's also given a guaranty of minimun income. He's allowed to vote the same as a partner. We call him a partner and advise the clients and others in the office

---

*This is not to be confused with participation in a qualified Profit Sharing Plan to be discussed in Chapter XII.

that he's à partner, BUT he doesn't own any proprietary interest (or stock) and is legally still an employee with a different salary set-up. If in the two year period he decides he wants out (as has happened) we terminate, but on termination there are no legal doings and undoings. He has not had to put up money since we didn't know until after a real trial whether we were for each other. I strongly recommend a two year profit sharing partner arrangement prior to the new lawyer being taken in as a true partner.

Then, if his two years as a profit sharing partner passes and all works well, bring him in as a true partner at a percentage agreeable to both parties. How do we handle this? Generally, in two stages.

Although the amount and method may vary somewhat, we generally have him buy his first smaller increment at a very low value. Why? We want him in. He's helped build the accounts receivable and so shouldn't have to pay for those at full value again. Also, once he's a partner he'll probably turn out more quality-profit production and be more economy minded. At this stage his partnership share won't be substantially greater than his former salary as a profit-sharing partner. The existing partners are not losing a large amount of income. So we let him in at far less than real value.

When he's ready to advance to a more full partnership, we make him pay for this added share at a more fully allocated cost. Why? Because the existing partners are now giving up a substantial piece of their action and while hopefully, the increased production and income the new partner will bring to the firm should balance his increased draw, there's always a risk. More so, the tangible assets are a real part of the older lawyer's ownership interest and it's fair that he be fully compensated as he starts to leave the firm.

Thus, we have a three-step progression from associate to partner:

- 2 years of being a "profit sharing" partner
- a buy in as a younger partner* at a lower cost than normally would be warranted
- an upward increase of interest at a full value

RULES:

1. Pick a partner who has a compatability of objectives, not the same style.

2. Bring him in early—right after you know he's for your firm permanently.

3. Use a profit sharing step prior to true partnership when first bringing in the new associate.

4. The first buy-in for a new partner should be at a lesser than full value.

5. The later step or steps to full partnership should be at more value.

---

*We never use the term "junior partner". It's demeaning.

VI
HOW TO LOOK FOR AN ASSOCIATE

or

It Doesn't Mean You Must Be Of The Same Mold

First, let's start with the premise that potential future associates will say anything they think you want to hear to get a job. So what do you look for? Not just a drone to do the garbage work and make money off of, but someone with whom you may someday want to be a partner. Reread the criteria for a partner in the previous chapter and see if you can be clairvoyant enough to find the intangibles in this new lawyer that you later look for in bringing him in as a partner.

How do we hire them? We pay $50-100 more per month than the going rate and clearly put them on a three-month, day-to-day trial basis. Why? Because interviews are a poor method of telling work habits and abilities. If they bomb you can get rid of them quickly before their name goes on the stationery, before they hang pictures or permanently antagonize your clients. In such case, do get rid of them quickly for their sake and yours. They may be good lawyers, but not for you. Split! We had one young lawyer for a short time who might have been excellent in his work product, but he had one eccentricity he couldn't break; he insisted on working all night from 9:00 or 10:00 p.m. to 6:00 or 7:00 a.m. All well and good, but when would we be able to discuss work product or memos? Where could we find him if we were on trial and needed immediate research work? He didn't fit.

But if they have the potential to fit into your partnership criteria keep them on; put them on your medical plans; inscribe their name in your records and WORK WITH THEM!

If one fits your criteria for a partner later, work with him on the day-to-day matters *more than you would normally.* If you train him to your office mode (not necessarily your legal style) it will pay dividends beyond belief later in money, time off and sharing of responsibility. To train an associate on a half-hearted basis and then fire him or have him leave is a waste of a substantial amount of your time. We've estimated that to train a young associate for 18 months costs us approximately $13,000 in excess of his production in overhead, partners', associates' and secretaries' time. So to terminate an associate is a severe cost in money and time. Put in *more* time and effort if the new associate has potential; it should pay back handsomely.

Earlier I said to initially overpay the going rate $50-100. Then, if he stays and you're happy with him keep $100 or more, plus fringes, ahead of the current going rate. This may sound philanthropic but it isn't, it's really selfish. By paying more, you increase the chance he'll stay and minimize the chance of his looking elsewhere; you're protecting your cash investment in him.

Always generously keep ahead of the going rate. It's an important investment in the overall stability and profitability of your firm. If you'll stop and think of the implication of generosity you'll realize that:

- you stand a better chance of employing and keeping a better qualified lawyer

- they are happier

- they won't leave as readily

- they'll work more diligently

- they'll be satisfied to work for you while you take a month off a year or an occasional sabbatical.

So, you say we're overly generous. OK! We think there's a good long range reason to be. But let's go further. We tell them in advance the fringes they are entitled to if they work out. As part of our "generosity" package we provide them in addition to their salary (and not from it):

- Participation in our Profit Sharing Plan and Pension Plan from the day he starts work (if he stays six months). Normally, this will mean an additional allocation to him equal to 20-25% of his salary.

- A month's vacation the second year as well as two weeks the first year.

- A Life Insurance Policy

- Health & Accident Policies

- A Salary Continuation Policy

The whole idea is to first determine your mutual satisfaction with each other and then keep him wedded to your firm.

RULES:

1. *Pick associates using the same criteria as you'd pick a partner.*

2. *Work closely with them and spend time.*

3. *Be overly generous. It'll be repaid.*

VII
HOW TO LOOK FOR A SECRETARY

or

She'll Run the Office Anyway,*
So Find Capable Ones

So what's the big deal about a secretary? Just phone the agency, interview a few, pick the best and pay the going rate. If you do that you are still wallowing in the philosophy of the lawyers of the thirties and forties (decades, not age). A secretary is such an integral part of the firm that you're foolish if you don't pay almost as much attention to picking a secretary as you would an associate.

We don't care about age. In fact, the skills we want, in addition to experience and ability, may favor an older woman. We don't care about looks as long as she's neat and

---

*Again with apologies to my daughter Lani, I'll use "she" in referring to a secretary, as most are. But one of the best secretaries of the four I've ever had was male.

presentable. My best and most long term secretary initially
described herself to me over the phone by saying "I'm five
by five." I said, "I don't want to chase you, I want to work
with you." Jean was a jewel.

We don't care if the proposed secretary has experience in
our speciality or even in the law. Preferable, yes, but not
required. We can train her. We want the more experienced
and stronger willed, if possible, for our younger associates.
They need all the help they can get and a secretary is an
ideal choice to be a greater helper and guide the younger
lawyer.

What do we look for in an interview and *checking* refer-
ences? The minimum good skills, of course, and the ability
to work with others. While each secretary works with a particular lawyer we frequently call on others and the secretaries frequently work together. So they must work compatibly
with others without the common "ours/yours" syndrome.
While you can never eliminate all the backbiting, many secretaries who work in a cooperative office realize the waste of
it and make an effort to minimize it; so we look for compatability (the same as an associate or future partner). We
look for a bright woman willing to learn as we're going to
turn her into a part-time paralegal assistant. Yes, I said
part-time paralegal assistant!

Now, when we've found her we pay her $50-100 *over* the
going rate. What difference! If she's no good or she's good
but doesn't work out, we terminate within three months so
the extra dollars are insignificant, but it shows her right
away we want quality and we're willing to pay for it. If she
stays with us "forever" we generally pay her $100-200 more
than the usual going rate which, together with fringes, has
two results:

> (a) It deters her from leaving us after we've spent time
>   and money in training her; and

(b) It's an incentive for her to learn more and help more and give the lawyer the opportunity for more time off.

Of course, she gets the same fringes as the associates and partners which sweetens the pot and furthers the above objectives. One of the fringes is that we don't want her to work on Saturdays, Sundays or nights, except in an absolute emergency, and if the emergency occurs more than once a month, your definition of emergency is too loose!

The average lawyer and firm may scheme to find ways to lessen her participation in the Profit Sharing Plan and Pension Plan or even cut her out of it completely; they may keep her salary low and other fringes at nil. I submit that such action results in inferior quality, faster turnover and assistance that makes you do work she could do for you just as well. You have time for more profitable pursuits. So our secretaries get their share of the Profit Sharing Plan and Pension Plan contributions (average $225 per month). They're covered by life, health & accident and wage continuation insurance, sick leave, and two or more weeks vacation a year. You may think us overly generous or even "nutty" but it's paid off in the quality and ability of those we have working for us and with us. They've helped make us money, so they should share in some of it.

Besides generous pay and benefits, we respect our secretaries' and receptionist's abilities to think as creative human beings. We encourage them to devise innovations and practices that will be more efficient and money saving *and we adopt them* when they're good. We've gotten some useful new techniques on the library, automatic typewriter use, and travel handling, to name but a few. We have meetings where these can be discussed and it's a source of pride and participation for them to offer and defend such an idea.

Now, you have a new secretary and she's studied—not

just read—the procedure manual. She's talked to the other women about the job and is working in well. She seems to have great possibilities. She's not a prima donna and not lazy and not a trouble maker. Let her work for about six months to get very familiar with your type of practice, your style and the office objectives, then start turning her into a *part-time paralegal.* She'll make your firm almost as much money as an associate, if she's really good.

Before going into some detail of what she can do for you as a part-time paralegal, let me explain why we use secretaries as such, rather than hiring and training full-time paralegals as many firms do. A paralegal is a "junior" lawyer. With several paralegals working in the office secretarial assistance is needed, space for one or two in an office is used and the proliferation of size and empire building is possible. I've already said we limit the size of our firm for cogent reasons; to increase it with full-time paralegals defeats this end. Others may find full-time paralegals of great value, and I admire that they've had the foresight to advance to this point, but we modify this by using secretaries.

In training the secretary to be paralegal, we spend time acquainting her with our specialty. We take her to occasional hearings or court. We have her sit-in while we abstract testimony of public witnesses, draft wills, handle incorporations, draft applications and pleadings, sometimes gather facts from clients, prepare verified statements and affidavits, and other documents of this nature. Later, she will do these herself, subject to our final checking over. All of this saves us the time to do other more complex and creative things that "pay" better money. While we may not charge the lawyer's full hourly fee for the secretary's time, the overall charge for her service far exceeds her total overhead and leaves considerable "profit." Try it if you can accept the fact that your non-law school trained secretary can truly do some of that kind of work, under your direction and supervision.

Don't use that old cliche, "but you're in a specialty and can do those things because. . . ." Recently on two occasions I've sat with contemporaries in general practice whose firms use paralegals as we do (except theirs are on a full-time basis). In both cases theirs were doing comparable work to ours. The difference is simply (a) we use ours part-time, and (b) train them ourselves.

Most of us at one time or another probably have been active in some Bar Association group or other public organizations of a philanthropic, civic or professional nature. I had always assumed from my own practice, that the lawyer's secretary did all the internal paper work that could be shifted to her; that she'd make arrangements for small or group lunches, for committee meetings, prepare mailings, prepare ballots, keep lists of payments, type minutes from my bare notes, handle scheduling and other efforts that she had the brains to do if the boss let her. I've been finding out that many lawyers do much of this phoning, dictating and paperwork themselves. At, for example, $70 per hour charge to the client, which results in a $35 per hour salary to yourself, why not let the secretary do it (at $7.50 per hour) and you do more of the $70 per hour work yourself? Let your ego get pride, not in your doing it yourself, but in having taught her how to do it.

The clients and other lawyers she'll sometimes be dealing with won't really be offended if she's tactful, if she makes it clear that you're tied up or in trial or out of the city and you don't want to hold this matter up, that she's getting the preliminary facts for you to work on. . . . No one has ever objected to expediting a matter that we are aware of.

I said earlier, we teach and train the secretary ourselves. That's true in the overall. But any course they want to take that may help us in the long run, we encourage them to take and we pay for it. Obviously, this includes any Bar Association sponsored Paralegal or Legal Secretary courses, but it also includes basic accounting courses, basic business law and wills and probate procedure courses (for lawyers). In our special field they've taken Interstate Commerce Commission Practitioners courses, which is for non-lawyers in the specialty, and three day Institutes given on our specialty. Every one of these helps broaden and advance their knowledge and makes them more valuable to us.

You ask where does she get the time to be part paralegal when she's also a full-time secretary? Over a period of years we've found that much of what a secretary did was (a) repetitious, or (b) unnecessary. In the first category we include effort that could be done better and faster in a simpler, more direct fashion. We try to save our office women all the time we can, so they can use it on more profitable production. On repeated letters, briefs, wills, and statements, we use the automatic typewriters; that cuts down on our secretarial time. Even here we didn't get a machine for each woman, but channel it through one secretary who is best suited to handle it, since it is a slight specialty in itself.

As to the "unnecessary" category, the office situation abounds with these. You get a one page typed letter, single spaced from an opposing lawyer or client asking for a "yes" or "no" answer. You sit down and either: (a) call your secretary in to take dictation, (b) put it on a dictating machine, or (c) write the answer out in longhand for later typing. She then goes through her ritual of typing it from the dictation or note, makes her copies for the file and other parties if they are involved, and mails it out. Why not just write on the original letter, "No, can't do!" and send a copy back to the sender and other involved parties—ten seconds instead of ten minutes. Your original shows on the upper right hand corner, "answered 10-2-77"; it shows a circle around the "cc:", which means you've clued in those involved; and more importantly, it went out fast. Further, our secretaries can use our receptionist to make the copies and type the envelopes; they only see it to know what's gone on. The original in our file, with our notations, is just as much proof of answer as an $8.30* investment in the secretary's time.

There are so many examples of this. Why send a formal transmittal letter just to transmit a copy of the other party's answer or other pleading when you can send a xeroxed answer and in black felt pen at the top write "any comments?"

The client won't think any less of you, probably more, when you break a little hide-bound tradition and save time. Maybe he'll even think it's going to cost him a little less!

RULES:

1. Again, be generous in paying a really good secretary, she's worth it.

2. Don't do anything yourself that she can do.

3. Train her to be a part-time paralegal.

---

*One recent estimate of the total cost of each letter we mail.

VIII
THE PROCEDURE MANUAL
or
Don't Confuse Me With Facts

Yes, a little firm of five lawyers has a Procedure Manual of 82 pages and 22 more pages of appendices! Sounds like an overkill, an ego trip, or a pompous exercise. Yet, if the large firms* find justification in the time and care of preparing and keeping one up, why not a smaller office having a more limited one? We find it a handy and now a necessary tool.

What is a Procedure Manual? It's first, a money saver; next, it is a written compilation of systems, practices, procedures, and rules that cover various facets of our business operation. It covers (as example only) our rules on vacation time, sick leave, termination pay, library upkeep, filing, retrieval, purchases and a myriad of other subjects, 58 in total at this point. We've attached to it a full job description of our receptionist, who is the "garbage dump" of the office, and the two overall functions handled by two of our secretaries—travel and automatic typewriter use. The fol-

_____

*I found a few of the larger firms don't even have one. Amazing!

lowing is a copy of the Table of Contents of our Procedure Manual to give you an idea of the subjects we cover.

TABLE OF CONTENTS

	Page
Introduction	I–IV
Advance fees and costs	1
Bank accounts	2
Banking procedures	3
Billing procedure and bookkeeping	7
Bills, payment of	8
Bonding	9
Calendar	10
Charge vouchers	11
Corporate minutes	12
Costs	14
Credit Cards	15
Files	16
File Memo (new)	17
Follow up Copies (Blue)	18
Forms	19
Holiday schedule	20
ICC applications (notes to secretaries)	21
ICC applications—calendaring	25
Insurance	26
Library	27
Lunch hours	35
Mail	36
Messenger	37
New clients, new cases, fees and bonuses	39
New employees	40
Office hours	41
Office meetings	42
Office Manager & Assistant	42(a)
Personnel Roster	43
Petty Cash	44
Pleadings procedure	45
Profit Sharing and Pension Plan—Clients	46
Promotion, entertainment and conduct Guidelines for Attorneys	47
PUC Applications	49
Reading file	50
Reference index system (X-file)	51
Rolodex	52
Safe and safe deposit boxes	53

Security 54
Sick pay 55
Style 56
Supplies 57
Telegrams 58
Telephones 59
Termination 61
Time sheets 63
Travel expenses and travel agency 64
Vacation pay 65
Wills 66
Xerox 67

Work description of Receptionist .... Appendix 1
Work description of Secretary
    responsible for Travel Arrangements .... Appendix 2
Work description of Secretary(ies)
    using automatic typewriter .... Appendix 3

Most offices not only don't have a Procedural Manual but they don't even have any rules. First let's answer why is it important? What are its purposes and benefits?

It's a time saver for the lawyers and therefore, a money maker for the firm. We don't have to constantly rehash the subject of the associates' and secretaries' vacation eligibility or priorities each year. Both are covered in the Procedure Manual in detail and unless changed by partnership action, are followed without constant re-evaluation.

Probably its greatest asset is the educational value for new employees. When most firms hire a new associate, secretary, receptionist, clerk, or bookkeeper, some one says "tell the new man/woman what to do." The quality of telling is normally bad, and may be wrong. The time it takes to do the telling is a substantial cost to the firm; and the telling may be wrong, biased, or both. After being hired and shown around the office, our new employee isn't told, "We'll see what work we can find you to start." Instead she's given a copy of the Procedure Manual to read and study; and this same worker will (hopefully) keep it and refer to it each time a new subject comes up, like priority of choosing lunch hours, which type of client costs to advance, how to retrieve stored files, and what goes on the master calendar. The total savings of time and money to us and our clients is staggering.

The same savings are made with seasoned employees, who should first refer to the Procedure Manual in resolving any problem or refreshing their memories. A listing of what current forms are available in the files, details of filing, the home addresses and phone numbers of the staff, and how to complete insurance forms and with whom to file them, are all down in black and white and need not lose something in retelling them from employee to employee.

The applicable uniformity of the rule to all employees is possible when it's written; it's no longer the prerogative of a partner to favor his secretary with special time off or a longer vacation. The uniform rule has been set after deliberation and thought and will be followed.

Conversely, it takes the partners "off the hook" to have it down in black and white. For example, the Procedure Manual says that except for new employees, salary review shall be made in December of each year. A more forward secretary, who has just done an excellent, heavy job, can't lean on her immediate boss for a quick raise, nor does she put him to the task of approaching his partners right then. The Procedure Manual provides the time. (Remember, our premise of Chapter VII is that she's generously paid, so she's not going to leave for that reason).

It's also some legal and practical protection. If an employee quits, and is disgruntled and should go to the "Labor Board" for claimed unpaid termination and/or overtime wages, we have a policy and practice on each subject spelled out in the Procedure Manual. We can prove these. Our only task is to show *as a policy* that we adhered to those rules for this one employee and past terminated ones. I'm not saying you'll always win, but we have never lost one.

In deciding whether to institute it, don't let task or size of a Procedure Manual deter you. How did we compile ours? One subject at a time over years. It started when I kept having various secretaries tell me what the rules should be for sick leave, termination pay and vacation pay. On occasions, they would play me against my partner or associate. So I wrote the rules down and put them in a file called "office rules"; Then as each new subject presented itself I, another lawyer or a secretary wrote it up; we went over it in detail and kept it in the file. We changed the language when warranted. We later put it in loose leaf; we added sections as the need came up, and still do. As to the form, the Table of Contents of subjects are kept alphabetically.

Then, one year when our receptionist was going on a longer vacation than usual, she *on her own initiative,* typed up a job description of the details of the various fifteen or so phases of her work, such as for example;

- How the file system is handled, including transfers
- How to physically handle the opening and in/out of the safe deposit box
- How she collects the data for the Master Calendar
- How she maintains and pays for the postage meter
- How the petty cash is handled

If she were to leave we wouldn't have to improvise and piece each task together for her replacement. Do you have any idea how much time that saves all parties? Time is money!

Changes in the Procedure Manual are frequent. They show some new thinking, and hopefully, improvement. In Chapter VII, I stated in part:

> " . . . *we respect our secretaries' and receptionist's abilities to think as creative human beings. We encourage them to devise innovations and practices that will be more efficient and money saving* and we adopt them *when they're good.*"

This holds true for the Procedure Manual. If an employee thinks of an improved idea or innovation, it's discussed and adopted in whole or part. The Procedure Manual rules are then modified and so not overlooked, forgotten or limited to use by just the one woman who suggested it. Uniformity again!

RULE:

Have a Procedure Manual. It's a necessity for every well run firm.

IX
FEES AND COSTS
or
Do Lawyers Always Overcharge?

This, and the chapter on Profit Sharing and Pension Plans are the most important when it comes to dollars ending up in your pocket. Yet, most lawyers pay less attention to the overall billing aspect than reconciling their home check book. Many of you consider it "grubbing" to even discuss it.

I cannot tell you how much an hour to charge, as that depends on many factors. I can tell you that whatever you charge you can make far more total money with the same scale by following a few of the rules set forth here.

First, let's explore how much you lose by failure to bill. Contrary to your usual belief, there is more than one step to billing*; there is more than just calling your secretary in,

---

*Obviously, some of this does not apply to cases handled on a contin-
gency basis.

dictating and then letting her worry about it. Each step means a possible loss of the billing unless a *fail-safe* method is used. You can't just dictate it or write it down and expect it will go out correctly. You can lose money by not getting the work on your time sheets or memos. If your secretary types a will or collects money for a client, where is the record of it on which billing is done? Certainly not your memory. You can lose billing by incorrectly assuming that another person in your office, who helped on the case, will do that billing. Did you ever investigate to determine whether your transcriber left off a $900 item you dictated when her boyfriend phoned her? Or, if you write separate billings on small pieces of paper, do you honestly know if you've ever lost one. Have you ever completed the billing, had it ready for mailing and then had one of the partners take one or two statements to hold "until the work goes out" or until he "can talk to the client about it"; it's possibly permanently lost or misplaced.

The point is that there are at least 5 or 6 times in the evolution of the billing process *when some billing might be lost, usually never to be regained.* A day or more work done by you with no remuneration is a loss from NET PROFIT, since the expenses keep on and on and on!

So we've instituted what we call our "fail-safe" method of billing. We know it's saved us a minimum of $400–500 average a month from one source. From the several sources it probably saves us $25,000 or more per year by plugging all leaks.* What's involved?

Step 1. One of our partners keeps a new business sheet loose leaf. It's rough and handwritten, but current and up-to-date. Every partner or associate may take in a case, so

---

*And remember that if that happens in our office where we are very business and profit conscious, how much do other offices "leak"?

how do we keep a central control for billing? Whenever a new matter is taken in, the lawyer advises the recording partner of it. There's no form or formality; it's usually by a small note paper with minimal information. The partner keeping the records enters it in the new business sheet in handwritten form;

Month	Client	Est. Fee	Type of Matter of Ident.
✓ Aug 77	Jones Truck	800	Incorporation
✓ Aug	Smith Tfr.	1900	Criminal Compl
1600 Aug	Gold Corp	3000	Civil Suit
220 Aug	Jones Truck	4000	ICC/PUC apps
✓ Aug	ABC Fixt	500	Tfr. Sale Business

In one place, therefore, we have listed chronologically all matters that come into the office. If a secretary takes in some collections by mail and handles them routinely, she makes sure it goes on the sheet. Even a casual will or phone matter is logged. Anything! Everything! Until the partner handling it checks off the matter on the left side it's still active and billable. It can't get lost. He has this new business loose leaf at our joint billing session (yes, I said "joint") and checks off when we finally bill a client or logs in in pencil an amount when we partially bill a client. It can't get lost. This new business sheet incidentally, has peripheral advantages in telling us: (a) the approximate amount of incoming business per month, (b) the type of business we're handling. This gives us a chance for long range planning.

Step 2. From our time sheets we dictate our detailed bills into a machine during a joint early morning session of *all* partners *and* associates. We know this is contrary to the practice of most firms, but I submit it has big advantages that more than pay for the time involved of all participants. Alphabetically we go through the clients' Time Sheet Register and bill all work done each month, making notes in red as to what's been billed to avoid duplicate billing in the next or future months. A red line is drawn at that session on the time sheets. If a bill was lost before mailing, we would be out that money unless we had further safeguards, which we'll discuss below. We also make sure our sessions are 3 to 5 days before the end of the month so that our bills can go out by the first. Most business firms will normally pay bills by the 10th; if ours is received later than that, we'll lose a whole month.

After the billing, but at the same session, the partner in charge of the above-described new business sheet goes down the list of unchecked or uncompleted items and rapidly brings to our attention any old items that are likely to have been forgotten, but are ripe for billing. I am not kidding you when I tell you that before this system at this stage and with this rudimentary reminder *we found an average of $400–500 per month of work done that never got on our time sheets and was overlooked and unbilled.* It's bound to happen to you if you don't use proper safeguards.

Parenthetically, this might be the best place to tell the reasons why we bill jointly; there are many. Joint billing means less is forgotten as one thought leads to another. Where two lawyers have worked on a matter they can bill between them, not both assuming the other will do the chore.

We achieve more uniformity by joint billing. On successful cases, some additional amount for result and responsibility can be added; in losing cases, some consideration can be made to cut it down. The poor financial position of the client may be known to one lawyer, while the one doing the billing is ignorant of it. A new partner can't give his services away cheaply in the hopes of building his clients closer to him. Consistency for like matters becomes the rule so the same client (or brothers-in-law) are not billed differently for similar work without cogent reasons. Jointly, we may remember something included in past billing that would have been wrongfully duplicated. During the billing sessions, one lawyer in charge of the "yellows" (office copies of past outstanding bills) keeps up with the rest, while reviewing these, and may briefly discuss collections of past due accounts and might even dictate "reminders" to clients.

Step 3. During the actual billing described in Step 2, one of the lawyers keeps a running summary on a small note pad that simply has client's name and amount billed. This is our next "fail-safe." When the bills are later drafted by a secretary and reviewed by various lawyers for correction, the one who keeps this "billing memo" *is the last one to go through the draft.* He checks them off to make sure the secretary didn't lose one in transcribing or inadvertently change an amount from $1,200 to $200 because she didn't hear the amount correctly. If there is a discrepancy the billing memo shows it and warrants a scrutiny as to "why." I cannot tell you how frequently wrong amounts are inserted *and never caught,* unless simple cross checks are made to the billing memo. Then the billing memo goes to the bookkeeper.

Step 4. Finally after typing, the bookkeeper brings back the final statements in sets, with the usual yellow copy (bookkeeper's) and blue copy (when it's a new billing and not just a rebilling). Again, after all the checking and review, the last one to handle is the partner with the "fail-safe" billing memo who checks them off. If any are missing because a partner is holding one or a secretary lost one, we can at least trace it down and it's not irretrievably gone. Our labor is preserved. That partner gives the sets of statements to the receptionist *and no one else* to: (a) mail the original, (b) gather the yellows for our account receivable file, and (c) gather the blues from which our bookkeeper enters new billing to the books.

The four steps may sound cumbersome or overly detailed, but they are not; they're easy and become automatic.

More importantly, they're worth the thousands of dollars that we harvest from the effort that otherwise would be lost. Don't be foolish enough to say, "I know our bills are never lost!" You don't know, and the chances are that some are lost.

I've mentioned use of time sheets. Whether your billings are preponderately on an hourly basis or not, these should be maintained. What do you do if a partner or an associate habitually fails to keep them or substantially fails to include his time. Well, he's cheating, not himself primarily, since he's getting a draw or salary, but all the rest. So we just cut off his draw or salary until he turns them in. If it continues, he becomes a *former* partner.

I've noted our bookkeeper's efforts several times. I automatically assumed every office centralized their billing of fees and costs. Yet, we know of several firms where EACH partner and his respective secretary sends their own bills to the clients for whom they worked, marks off part or full payment as checks are received and rebills delinquent amounts. This is inconceivable, but it happens. The loss of revenue, favored lower billing, missing costs, lack of accuracy and chance for chaos is appallingly clear. Yet, often they continue.

I didn't think I had to mention that we bill monthly, but because many firms still bill quarterly, less frequently, or "when they feel like it," something should be said. It's a rich firm that can stand to finance their clients, but worse, it's a gambling firm that doesn't bill monthly. A client is far more apt to accept smaller, more frequent bills than fewer ones of larger amounts. This is true even of large corporations, since human being comptrollers on limited salaries have to approve those bills. Also, the client is far more cognizant of your worth, the closer the billing is to the actual work done. The client's "Curve of Gratitude" peaks at the point (a) where he needs you most, and (b) where you perform the most vital, visual service. After that, it's downhill. Why not let him be happy to pay your bill by submitting it at the peak—monthly, when you did the work?

Initially, in this chapter I said, "I cannot tell you how much an hour to charge, ...," but, I can give you one maxim (over all others) that will allow you to raise your fees.

Have you any idea which one factor influences a client's views concerning the fairness of your fee? Results? Time spent? Speed? Prestige of the law firm?—None of these, strangely. *It's the factor of the client being kept informed.*

In my 30 years of practice I've taken literally scores of lawyers' business courses, read hundreds of office management and fee billing books and talked to hundreds of clients; I agree with others who have concluded that the most important, single aspect of the client satisfaction is whether his lawyer kept him informed of all the phases of his problem.

How many lawyers take a case and assume that as long as it's moving (even slowly) the client will be satisfied? How many lawyers complain of a client constantly phoning to find the status of his case? The simple remedy is the informed client.

We have an office rule that a copy of every letter, memo, research or pleading prepared in the office by us, or received from others, goes to the client unless we specifically denote otherwise. The informed client is happier and more satisfied—and more *billable!*

Some discussion about hourly billing and bonus arrangements should be made. A substantial majority portion of our efforts are billed on an hourly rate. If this were 100% true, however, we could eliminate various procedures and safeguards and use computerized billings. But there are

many human variants (see Step 2 above) that we feel mili-
tate against computer billing for us. Hence, the joint billing
technique.

Also, we handle some cases on a bonus basis which depend, in part, on results attained. It's our belief that the
bonus arrangement is an ethical continuing incentive *for
both sides.* We use it for larger cases where our moving party
is seeking something of value. We use it where we act as a
broker in bringing people together or finding them the
deal. Most clients do not object to a bonus-type arrangement particularly when they need and want you at that
moment. They calculate the cost in as part of the deal or
results, but you must discuss it with them in advance of
starting work and long before billing is done. When we use
it, we do so only when: (a) the client is fully aware of it, and
(b) it's in writing between us. Don't ever leave it to chance or
memory. I remember one case that after 4½ years lapse we
won the case and billed the bonus agreed upon (in addition
to our current monthly bill). The president complained that
no bonus had been agreed upon, she had even checked
with her predecessor who "had sworn on his children's
heads" there was no such arrangement. I simply sent my old
letter outlining the agreement which had been signed and
accepted by the executive officer; back came a check in full.
The few disputes we've had over bonus billings have been
when we failed to reduce to writing the agreement. Often
the client's memory is short. Make sure you have the written
means to refresh it.

Another thought on billing and fees. I've assumed
throughout that each statement includes detailed, proper,
billable costs laid out for the client. Does yours?

Preliminarily, we don't ever charge them for secretaries'
overtime (on the few necessary occassions it occurs), notary
fees, taxi costs, automobile mileage on short trips in the area
or local area toll calls. They might be properly chargeable

items, but there is a line at which clients claim "cheapness." We were once given a case taken from a very large law firm who billed the client on some of these costs. The client was incensed. He didn't mind the $17,000 in fees charged him, but objected to a total of $46.45 for taxis, filing, notary fees and secretaries' overtime, so we absorb those type of costs. We also limit our daily chargeable, out of town hotel and travel costs and charge only for tourist flights. If we want to travel in better style that's fine, but we absorb it so as not to make the client feel we're better than he. Empathy is discretion of a sort.

As to recovering costs we have set up a workable system to bill out those costs that can legitimately be passed on to the client, without losing the cost, in the shuffle or (as above) antagonizing the client. I cannot stress how much money most offices lose through carelessness and failure to keep records. Have you any idea of the various categories of items that are properly recoverable? Just to name a few:

Long distance telephone	Telegrams
Filing fees	Heavy mailings
Travel expenses	Air freight
Reproduction Costs	Courier
Corporate sets	Airline ticket
Incorporation sets	

The point is that a great drain on most offices is the failure to recapture costs advanced for clients. Of course, we have systems to minimize the losses as you do; but we enforce and constantly improve ours. What percentage of your long distance calls are rebilled? If it's not 99% you're giving money away. Are all of your lawyers travel expenses finding their way into clients' statements or are some lost en route? When you have heavy, chargeable mailings for a particular client, an air express or courier package, or a large Xerox job, does the person handling it forget to make a charge slip? These losses are not an overhead increase, but a direct net loss to PROFIT. You are probably losing $950 per month (as I'd estimate in a five man firm); that's a total of almost $12,000 per year. What's your partnership percentage of that loss that you're giving away? 15%, 20% or 25%? That is a nice vacation lost for you and the family by simply not keeping an efficient business-like store, by not keeping complete track of billable costs. That's a big personal penalty.

Also, on this subject is the clients unwarranted assumption that you will advance his filing fees and other charges, and your stupidity in doing so! You're a lawyer, not a banker. In our practice formerly we advanced charges for filing applications, complaints, incorporations and corporate sets; we found we had a sum sometimes equal to 25% of an average month's fee billings for such advanced costs. Thereafter we instituted a rigid policy of requiring the client to pay these charges in advance. Whenever we forwarded a document for filing we asked for a return check to the appropriate office for the amount of the filing fees. When we ordered transcripts they came with the bill for services. Now, on non-contingency cases, we order the transcripts asking that the bill go directly to the client—and he pays it.

There were no complaints and we went out of the banking business. Embarrassing? Demeaning? Absolutely not. Look at the cash we released to ourselves.

Perhaps last to be discussed is our collection policy. Our clients paid their employees weekly and their suppliers monthly. They paid their own wages and bonus promptly, but our bills were frequently long delayed. Those creditors of this same client who asked often and loud received money. "A squeeky wheel gets oiled." We were carrying 4-6 month's accounts receivable. Horrendous! After going into the question carefully and researching it from the ethical and public relations standpoint we added a finance charge to all amounts unpaid after 30 days and advised our clients of this. Result:

(a) We lost no clients whatever.

(b) We cut our accounts receivable dramatically— in half—down to two months total, or less.

We continue to advise all clients of this by a simple, printed disclosure statement on the lower portion of our statements. Just calculate the interest saved on such accounts receivable not carried. It's profit!

RULES:

1. *Bill jointly if size of firm allows; if not, bill jointly within departments.*

2. *Put in fail-safe methods to avoid losing legitimate and proper billing of work done while it works its way through various hands.*

3. *Send monthly statements.*

4. *Don't finance your clients by advancing their costs or letting accounts receivable build up.*

X

IS SPEED ESSENTIAL IN ALL CASES?

or

Only If You Want A Greater Profit

Be honest with yourself; is the speed with which you handle matters for the client's benefit, or for your own benefit? Do you manage his legal affairs in a reasonably prompt and expeditious manner, or instead, do you frequently delay them in order to handle other cases?

The precept we follow in our office is "Do it Now!"

We follow that rule for two basic reasons:

- It's fair, best and least expensive for the client.

- It's far more profitable for our firm.

In an earlier chapter I talked of the procrastination of a lawyer, or firm, in not putting their own affairs in order. It's a sad habit. Let's now direct ourself to the dollar sav-

ings that a lawyer can make for himself and his firm by
following the maxim, "Do it Now!"

Stop and take out some of your still active old routine files
and examine them. If only in a brief, cursory, non-business
way, examine them to determine:

- In a will file: after your client discussed the matter with you completely and thoroughly, did
  you put the file aside, forget the details and
  later have to meet with him again to "go over
  some thoughts I have"?

- In a typical lawsuit pending in court: Did you
  delay the filing of the complaint because you
  had to meet with the client again when you
  "forgot" some of the detail he had given you?
  Did you delay because other cases that later
  came in needed work done? Or are there constant delays from lawyers' stipulations extend-
  ing time for their own benefit? Are there mutu-
  ally agreed delays of motions, preconference
  hearing, settlements and trials?

- When you have received an important letter:
  Do you sometimes put it on the bottom of the
  pile to answer later? Does it ever get delayed
  even if it's routine? Do you ever delay giving it
  to a young associate who will then delay the
  research required? Do you then delay the meeting with the client to give him the final results or
  opinion?

- In collecting money for a client: Do you delay
  the letter writing? The follow-up? The filing of
  suit or referral out to an agency or other lawyer?
  Or the payment of the money to the client when
  it is collected?

- In domestic relations cases (or others): Besides

all the other built-in delays, do you make it a habit to do nothing until the client calls you to move it along?

• In handling incorporations: How fast are you in meeting the client when he wants to go ahead? Do you delay giving him the checklist of data required to move ahead? When you get that data do you delay the preparation (and filing) of the Articles of Incorporation? Worse yet, do you first do the Articles, then later the minutes and By-Laws, then later yet, the stock filings? Couldn't they have been done all at the same time while the matter is fresh in your mind?

• And when it comes to (most matters) ... ask yourself if you aren't often the major cause of an overall delay!!

The client is entitled to expedited service. Not instant service, but expedited. Not to give him this entitlement robs him of (a) the extra cost inherent in the delay, and (b) a resolved matter for the deferred period. The lawyer delays. The lawyer's public image is bad. Isn't it understandable that the public has been ridiculing and chastising lawyers for years? Justice appears not only blind, but slow. We see manifestations of the public's confidence in us in self-help books on "HOW TO ..." in the fields of divorce, incorporation and drawing wills. I know part of the reason is attributable to legal costs, but that's not all of it.

More important, for purposes of this discussion, is the extra cost to you, the lawyer. Part of the delay that you build into these cases *is paid for by you.* You cannot pass along the full cost of the time for every stipulated delay to plead, or postponement of a hearing, or trial. If you do it's not fair to the client. When you absorb it, or any part of it, you lessen your profit. If you are on a contingency or a fixed set fee, you absorb it all.

Recently two different cases were brought into our office by other attorneys who, for varied reasons, wanted us to handle the cases. I personally investigated the file time sheets and billing on each. I found on the first a total of $3,200 billing to date, of which $475 was directly attributable to delays, redone work from the delays and time spent on calls, meetings and agreements with other lawyers to postpone. I found on this same case that the lawyer had absorbed approximately $350 in time for the same reason. Thus, the client and lawyer lost money. The second case was almost as bad.

The traditional reasons and excuses for the delays are legion and perhaps as varied as the number of lawyers you speak with. But the results are:

- unfairness of delay to the client

- extra cost to the client

- extra cost to the lawyer

Bluntly put, if you are too busy to move your work expeditiously, you shouldn't be taking in new cases. Yes, I said that seriously. If you can't do it fast, don't take it! You are not doing your client justice; you're not helping the public image of lawyers; and you're not maximizing your profit by taking in too much work, but minimizing it. You're costing your client legal fees because you are taking in more work than you can reasonably handle.

I might parenthetically remind you that in Chapter IV we discussed upgrading your practice, i.e., terminating our relationship with those clients and cases that aren't suitable for you to handle profitably. The result was giving better service on the cases you keep. That means cut down the delay you build into those cases.

The lawyer shrugs off the fact that he can't bill in some matters until they are completed: Collections, suits for sums on which there is a contingency, incorporations, mergers and some sales. There are other matters that the heavier billing is at the end of the line. Your delaying the case delays receiving your fee.

What maxims do we follow to avoid the constant delays? We have a built-in rule, "Do it Now". We train ourselves and our associates to assiduously avoid delays; we do not take in more work than we can do expeditiously.

These may be just words to you. Brave philosophy, but not specifics. OK, let's give a few specifics of *how* we expedite our work and make more money doing it.

We never ask for extensions on deadlines unless absolutely necessary for the client's benefit, not ours. We insist on meeting deadlines even if they are self-imposed, not court imposed. We don't allow other lawyers to have more than *one* extension; yes, they have to go to a court, over our opposition, to get it. We purposely promise a client a definite time for his will, corporation, complaint, or application, to be ready; that puts a pressure on us to keep our promise—and our habit intact. We use speed letters that we can send out almost as we read some of the letters to be answered. Or as detailed in Chapter VII, we answer the incoming letter in handwriting right on the face of it and get it out the same day. We interchange matters with comparable or even more experienced lawyers, if the one otherwise regularly handling it goes on vacation, has another trial, or is busy.* For several reasons, including the last, we insist on a uniform system of filing so any lawyer or secretary can get into the file quickly; and we insist on all files being up-to-date and in excellent order for the same reasons.

We do legal work on one matter as completely as possible

---

*More of this in detail later. See Chapter XIV.

at one sitting, rather than only the minimum necessary to move it to the next step; it's fresh in our mind and we can do it quicker overall. For example, in an incorporation, we do the Articles, By-Laws, First Minutes, Stock Permit application, and all other phases, at one sitting, even if we aren't going to send them all out right then; or in an adoption case, we completely draft or finalize the petition, orders, services and other required papers at one time. We're going to have to do them anyway; many are pro forma and routine. It's fresh in our mind and we can always modify them, if necessary.

So why not do in volume that which you can? You will charge the client the same either way. Even in a civil complaint case, if you know you're going to ask interrogatories at a later stage, why not draft them at the time you get your client's facts; they're fresh in your mind and you can add to them later, as you learn more.

We also use another technique alluded to in the Chapter on Fees (Chapter IX). We constantly keep our client informed on every aspect of the matter being handled. Why do I mention it here? Because it's a great prompter to moving his matter along. He gets a copy of every pleading, every letter, every memorandum, every research, every stipulation of order; everything! If he sees an unnecessary pause, he might himself timidly (or forcefully) follow it up with you. It's an external prod to us. But also, the client being kept informed, minimizes repeated telephone calls as to "what's doing"? Some of these calls, while never charged for —and thus, absorbed by the lawyer—are time consuming. Less profit.

We prod and push each other. At our billing sessions, monthly meetings, and lunches, we inquire as to status. This expedition becomes self-fulfilling from pride (or fear) if for no other reason.

Delay of the clients' cases costs us money, besides being unfair and costly to them. We're oriented to a profit so we expedite.

RULES:

1. The client is entitled to expedited service.

2. Such service makes the lawyer more money.

XI
CORPORATE OR PARTNERSHIP*
or
There Really Is No Choice

If you are looking at the overall profitability for yourself and expect to make money in your law practice, then, in my opinion, you should incorporate.** The tax and non-tax advantages by far outweigh the disadvantages. At least if you analytically and purposely decide not to incorporate you've made a choice; but I know for a fact that many of our sisters and brethren do not incorporate because of inertia, old-fashioned concepts, procrastination or fear of the unknown. They are giving money to Uncle Sam as the stiff penalty.

We've been incorporated since California allowed professional corporations. We have purposely reviewed that

---

*Here, in this chapter, the use of "parties," "shareholders," or "corporation" will be used precisely.

**Besides your state law prohibiting incorporation, the only possible exception might be if you are a sole practitioner; even then I have my doubts on not incorporating.

decision, and had outside tax and business consultants impartially do the same for us. Without dissent, there is unanimous corroboration of that eight year old decision.

Let's discuss the advantages from two views:

- Tax benefits; and non-tax advantages

- Qualified Profit Sharing Plan/Pension Plan. (It may be considered a taxable benefit, but it's major so I put it in a separate category)

Some Tax Benefits. The benefits ennumerated below are primarily tax benefits, but may also include non-tax benefits in many cases.

If you are a partner, no deduction is allowed for group term-life insurance premiums paid by you, but, as an employee (and as a shareholder), premiums on life coverage up to $50,000 are deductible to the corporation. If you need more than the $50,000, you get a further break since you personally are taxed not on the corporation's actual premium payment, but on the Treasury's artificial table of insurance costs. It's in effect discount insurance. With both these benefits the overall saving is perhaps $1,000 a year.

All costs in group medical insurance, hospitalization and accident & health plans are deductible to the corporation and not taxed to you. These could save you about $1,200 or more a year. This is far better than you, as a partner, taking premiums paid as a personal medical deduction—if you can qualify to take it.

The corporation can elect to provide your wife or estate with an excludable death benefit up to $5,000 free of estate or income tax. As a partner you can't do so. The savings could be up to $2,500 or more, depending on the size of your taxable estate.

The professional corporation can provide reimbursement for all medical and dental expenses of selected employees including you, on a discriminatory basis; this can also be provided to your dependents at the election of the corporation. Certainly your legal partnership can't do that. This savings depends on such varying factors it can not readily be calculated.

Both a tax and non-tax benefit is the coverage afforded to you by "your" corporation of Workers' Compensation, social security and state disability insurance. Two of these are deductible to the entity since you are a legitimate employee. As a partner or sole proprietor lawyer, they are either not deductible, or, if so, only on a limited basis under certain circumstances.

By choosing a corporate fiscal year different than the shareholder's own, there can be some shifting of income from a higher to a lower bracket. There are many variants of this in using tax techniques. Prudent planning can legitimately and effectively lessen taxes over a two year or longer period.

Further, it is a direct benefit to the corporation and its shareholders to realize that income is taxed at a more favorable 20% rate on the first $25,000 of taxable income and 22% of all taxable income over $25,000; with the 26% surtax rate only applying on taxable income over $50,000 per year. This normally compares with far higher individual rates had that amount been fully paid out to the shareholders employees in addition to their salaries.

Perhaps not quite measurable, is the so-called "double-pocket" concept of both your corporation and you individually filing returns. Office, promotion, entertainment, automobile, telephone, parking, business travel, and other expenses can be reimbursed by the corporation to you; but, if not reimbursed, they can frequently be deducted personally as legitimate business expenses expended in pursuit of your vocation.

Non-Tax Benefits. There are more benefits to the shareholders from corporate existence; there are several of a non-tax type. I discount limited liability as being, in the overwhelming number of cases, of no moment (and usually so circumscribed as not "limited"), but it's a factor.

The ease of transfer of stock interest on death or withdrawal is apparent. Picture yourself handling a client's estate and making a determination of which is easier to clear up, a partnership interest or stock ownership.

I've already alluded to the tax benefit of the corporation deducting and providing social security and Workers' Compensation to you, as well as mandatory inclusion in your state disability insurance program; but the benefits beyond taxability consequences are real. They can amount in California, for example, to about $1,800 per year, plus a possibility of death proceeds under Workers' Compensation.

We think there is an advantage to the streamlined business administration of a corporation over a partnership. You must and should want to keep the corporation separate from the partner's personal business for many reasons. This has an advantage in orderly handling without one partner taking undue advantage. In firms having constant turnovers, it's easier to handle; in day to day management it is easier. Problems concerning the separation of assets between partners is minimized or eliminated by corporate ownership.

Voting control can be separated from the ownership of stock in a corporation, but is difficult or sometimes impossible in a partnership. Voting trusts, revocable or even irrevocable proxies may be granted. If you are a selling senior shareholder you can sell your stock over a period of time, but retain a measure of say as a protection. Conditional proxies can be utilized for you as a retiring shareholder or to younger members coming up the line. The stock as a retiring shareholder can be held without voting interest; but it may have a real value in coverage of malpractice insurance, long-term payout, or other cogent reasons. The important point being that there's more flexibility in handling shares than in having a partnership interest.

Deferred compensation to you as a specific lawyer employee may be arranged upon a discriminatory basis. This is in addition to the qualified pension plan we'll discuss in the next chapter. Thus, the corporation may agree with you to make continued payments to you after you retire or even to your family in case of your death. All or part of this is deductible to the corporation. It may result in lessening your income during otherwise higher tax bracket periods and receiving income later when you are in a lower bracket.

Profit Sharing and Pension Plans Advantage.* Here I wish I could wax eloquent as I believe this advantage alone equals or exceeds all the rest. *We have in our firm both allowable plans and contribute the maximum allowable amount.*

All contributions to your qualified plans are deductible to the corporation and not then taxable to the beneficiaries. As a rule of thumb, that can be up to 25% of the total earnings of all participants. So you say, "But, I don't have that much (or any) left to put in."

---

*In the next chapter I'll describe in more detail some tax savings, the set up and administrative organization; also, I'll briefly compare it with Keogh.

Then I say:

- read this book again thoroughly and by following its precepts, save yourself more money than that;

- cut the salaries of all the partners and contribute that amount instead of trying to save outside the plans; or

- go into some other business because you're not business wise suited to be a lawyer.

Why is this so important? Taxable corporate income in excess of $50,000 is taxed at 48% for federal purposes plus usually a further percentage for your state income taxes. If you pay it out in salaries at the top bracket it's usually close to 50% federal—again, plus state taxes. *Instead,* if left to accumulate in the plans *without the tax bite* and drawn later, you'll either be retired or semi-retired and in a much lower bracket.

It can be your security in retirement.

One dramatic effect of tax free accumulation and compound interest (presented on a simplistic basis) will here suffice. Assume you earn $75,000 a year from your practice, of which you save—in one form or another—$7,500. You pay more than 50% income tax to both IRS and your state, so the $7,500 you save comes from $15,000 gross earnings before taxes. This is especially true since it's the last dollars and at the highest bracket. Assuming your after tax investment earns an average of only 5% per year, your savings outside the Plans will accumulate at the rate of only 2½% net after taxes. Thus, $7,500 invested for 25 years at 2½% will give you a nest egg of $240,000.*

---

*This doesn't take into effect the higher taxes you might pay on the income from your investments in later years. For simplicity I've used a straight 50% tax.

If, however, you use the full $15,000 *before taxes* and invest it through the plans, then the corporate income and your spendable remains unchanged, since it's deductible to the corporation and not taxable to you at that time. Since the plans pay no income tax, the 5% earnings accumulate in full and will work for you at 5% instead of at 2½% net. At the end of the same 25 years, you'd have approximately $715,000 instead of $240,000. Quite a $475,000 difference on which to later pay lower taxes.

I also recognize that there are some disadvantages to the corporate form, but submit that these are either not major or with careful handling, avoidable. Less immediate cash and start-up costs are some reasons lawyers permanently defer the choice and transition. The extra costs of FICA, Workers' Compensation or state disability insurance, may actually be to your advantage as above-described. The extra costs of Franchise Tax (State Income Tax), malpractice insurance, or maintenance of your corporation are a small trade-off for the enormous benefits derived. The possible legal risks and problems of unreasonable salary to shareholders, collapsible corporations or accumulated earnings, have not appeared. Those that braved them early were well rewarded. Those that have waited to start have lost the past years' benefit of accumulation.

Well, that's it in a simplistic form. We've lived with it, perused the advantages and disadvantages of corporate form and use of Profit Sharing Plan/Pension Plan and review it constantly. There's little reason for us to change our minds when we see our future retirement build and build and build.

RULES:

1. Practice in a corporate form.

2. Use the qualified Profit Sharing Plan/Pension Plan forms of retirement benefits.

XII
PENSION AND PROFIT SHARING PLANS
or
We Never Missed A Beat

I said in the last chapter that the biggest tax advantage of a corporate set-up is the Pension and Profit Sharing Plans. I'll say it another way: It's the biggest and best tax shelter and money maker that the average lawyer can have for himself.

In our view, it's a MUST!! I can't be stronger than that.

The genius combination of compound interest *and* minimizing taxes warrants some of the few drawbacks we'll talk about in a minute.

In comparing participation and non-participation in a plan(s), I'm assuming (a) a lawyer employee not having a qualified plan(s) taking his gross available distributive salary and investing 20%* of what is left *after tax payments* versus

---

*20% referred to overall is the same as 25% of the salary actually paid to the employee-shareholder, which 25% will either be (a) saved individually, or (b) contributed to the plan.

(b) the comparable lawyer being paid 80% of that cash available by the corporation, as salary, with the other 20% being contributed by the corporation to the plans.* Over 10, 15, 20, or 25 years it makes a huge difference. The following calculations of comparisons are dramatic and should help convince you of the need for you and your co-shareholders, to have both qualified plans:

RESULTS OF QUALIFIED PLAN VS. NO PLAN

Annual Gross Taxable Income Average Over 25-Year Period	No Retirement† Plan; Total Amount of 25-Year Accumulation After Taxes	Retirement Plan; Total Amount of 25-Year Accumulation After Taxes	Total 25-Year Tax Savings° Attributable to Retirement Plans
$ 25,000	$176,421	$ 240,171	$ 63,750
50,000	298,255	480,342	182,087
75,000	369,168	720,513	351,345
100,000	457,635	960,684	503,049
125,000	547,763	1,200,855	653,092

Thus, a lawyer with a net income of $50,000 over a 25-year period could accumulate retirement assets of $480,342° under qualified retirement plans. Without the plans, with only savings after-tax dollars, he would for the same period, accumulate only $298,255. As the tax bracket increases the savings increase in greater proportion.

Lest you think that the huge savings must be left over a 25-year period, let's look at it from the stand-point of a

---------------------- ⌡

*I recognize that the corporation doesn't contribute the lawyers specific money, nor is any designated portion of the contribution attributable from a specific employee.

† The assumptions made are: A 20% savings of available cash per year over a 25-year period, which is equal to 25% of salary taken and spent; 5% accumulation rate; married taxpayer; with two children; reasonable deductions each year; 1977 rates; no state taxes included or deducted. Also the calculations are based on the taxes paid at on overall income.

°Less taxes paid at a later date at a probable lower tax bracket.

lawyer in his mid-forties who may have (or only want) to work 15-20 years more. Under the same assumption, let's look at the savings of plans versus no plans for only 17 years more of practice.

RESULTS OF QUALIFIED PLAN VS. NO PLAN

Annual Gross Taxable Income Average Over 17-Year Period	No Retirement Plan; Total Amount of 17-Year Accumulation After Taxes	Retirement Plan; Total Amount of 17-Year Accumulation After Taxes	Total 17-Year Tax Savings Attributable to Retirement Plans
$ 25,000	$100,916	$130,241	$ 29,325
50,000	174,160	260,282	86,122
75,000	225,691	390,723	165,032
100,000	282,309	520,964	238,655
125,000	339,956	651,205	311,249

Of course, there is a tax on the money received later from the plans, but it should be at a lower rate. Also, it's assumed you'll earn more as time goes on and so your savings shown above will probably be much greater.

But, I beg you, if you go into it, use both plans and put in the maximum allowable. Look at the figures!

If you're not yet convinced and say, "But I don't—and can't—save," then I say, "more reason to have these plans!" It's a discipline you may well need, and, they *may be your only retirement savings plans.* It's a wholesale savings method and you get the benefit of buying dollars at a big discount. If you could buy AT&T stock each month at a 50% discount and pay taxes "later", would you do it? Of course. It's the same here.

I know there is Keogh (H.R. 10) to consider. It used to be so bad when the limit was $2,500 that it was of little use, but the only thing available. Now with a $7,500 maximum, it's more attractive. We found too many drawbacks, particularly for the higher paid lawyers; and what lawyer, even when

young, doesn't aspire eventually to move into that category?
There are disadvantages:

- Keogh has a $7,500 limit compared to a rule of
  thumb 25% contribution (plus forfeitures of
  others in the qualified Profit Sharing Plan).

- Unused deductions in Keogh are lost, whereas,
  in qualified plans they are carried over.

- H.R. 10 requires immediate full vesting when
  the other employees are eligible, rather than a
  period of partial vesting.

- Keogh is fully taxable on death, whereas, the
  qualified plan has better tax treatment.

- The investment media of Keogh is much more
  restrictive than the other.

- The employee lawyers cannot act as a Trustee
  under Keogh though they may under the corporate plan.

- Employees may not borrow from an H.R. 10
  fund, while they may do so under a qualified
  plan.

- There may be better tax treatment under a
  coporate plan of distributions in a single year on
  retirement by income averaging than under
  H.R. 10 rules.

- The age of retirement under qualified plans is
  more lenient and flexible.

I recognize there are some disadvantages in these plans,
but they are slight. Of course, you must take in other employees besides the lawyers; that includes your secretary,
receptionist or others working over 20 hours a week. If you
provide a 10-year vesting schedule and employees leave
after 2 to 4 years, they'll take with them only 20 to 40% of
their share. The balance in the Profit Sharing Plan goes to

you and the others remaining; the balance in the Pension Plan goes to lower next year's contributions. One of the plans can be integrated with social security; your being in a higher bracket will give you even more proportionately than otherwise. Another disadvantage is the added reporting and details of qualified plans under ERISA. But these aren't onerous. For an inexpensive and reasonable amount, our most capable administrator, Bakewell & Company* handled all of it with no effort on our part.

You are now convinced and want to start one or both plans. Start both and *exert every effort to put in the maximum* even if it means cutting the shareholder employee salaries a little or redirecting your present savings policy. When you see it accumulate, tax free, you'll be ecstatic in five years that you did.

Let's discuss how we started ours. Formerly, when we handled all types of practice, I participated as a lawyer in the formation of over 25 plans for clients. In this day of changing tax rules, new laws and specialization, we had determined that our clients, and us, would be better served by hiring a professional administrator. We did and have been happy with the choice ever since. Grant Bakewell took us easily through the discussion of various options, preparation of the plans, IRS submission and qualification, and even supplied us with forms of minutes and other required documents. He charged less by far than if we ourselves could had done it for ourselves. Our time is MONEY to us. They now do the yearly actuarial reports, year end allocation and vesting details, and keep us up-to-date. One less headache for very little cost that saves us our time to devote to higher paying clients' matters.

One other reason for using an outside specialist to set it up for you,—*It'll get done.* One of our lawyer friends has

---

*And they didn't even reduce our charges for this unsolicited plug.

talked of it for six years and recently finally "got to it"; but they lost valuable five years of compounding their savings and the tax deductions. An outsider would have done it before the end of the first fiscal year.

Most every plan is different and must be tailored to meet your own needs, so it's foolish of me to counsel what yours should include. I'll comment only on a few of the more salient points that mean money in your pocket.

First, we constantly contribute the maximum allowed by law, which is roughly 25% of the salaries of all participants. We do this for reasons earlier stated. It is like buying money wholesale; but we deposit it *monthly* directly into the accounts exactly *as if we were paying rent or salaries.* It thus becomes a monthly obligation. For example if the total monthly salaries of a three lawyer office (including secretaries and receptionist) are $15,000, then $3,500–4,000 should be put aside monthly for the two plans. It is easier this way and becomes habit forming.

As to employees' participation, we are liberal. You can wait a year, or in some cases slightly more for them to come into the plans; we provide for only a 6-month wait. Once employees are included you can vest their interest over a 10-year period. We provide, instead, for 20% per year to be vested. As I stated earlier, we try to pick top quality employees (they make more money for us) and encourage their staying (it saves retraining new ones). Thus, we use our plans as incentives to make more profit.

When we started our plans, we picked our regular bank as the Trustee for both Plans and were satisfied. However, since we have our own resources to pick and select the investments, the Bank, in effect, became only a custodian for the securities. We later became Trustees and save considerable money for the Plans; but if you are not doing your own selection, give serious thought to a Bank Trustee. We, instead chose an advisor-consultant* to work with us on a monthly meeting basis, and, between us, decide on the purchase and sale of the investments. This is a personal matter. The advisor can be an investment counselor, a bank trust office, a top quality stock broker, or anyone who knows what he or she is doing.

In our eighth year of our Plans we have done well—not spectacularly. Even after taking into consideration (a) our earlier speculative flings and (b) the 1973–74 poor market, we have increased our values over 10% per year *compounded yearly.*

Since this is a book about how YOU can make money, let me give you our formula which has been successful. It's your nest egg, your retirement, your future. Whether you are a self-trustee or use a Bank, it is worth time to oversee the management of it. Here's the regimen:

- Our advisory committee, at least two of our three lawyers, meets with our stock consultant every month (formerly when we had a corporate trustee, its representative was included). The meeting is usually an hour long and may take place at lunch. We discuss, review and decide. Even if we feel in advance that we will probably do nothing that month, we meet. It's a discipline and group therapy to have us control the plans instead of drifting. Even though we put money away every month and meet every month, we don't have to buy every month. That's a discipline also. We let the cash grow in Treasury Bills, Insurance Notes or a savings account until we

---

*Donald W. Davis of Davis Skaggs Co., Inc. Don has done such an excellent job he should charge us more money. On the other hand, my giving him a plug should give us reduced commissions and charges.

feel we have the right purchase. This has ben-
efited our portfolio—and our learning patience.

- We receive from our broker a monthly computer
  runout with all data on each Plan. This is used at
  our monthly meeting and informs us of our
  status.

- We never (but never) order the Trustee to buy or
  sell based on a "doorway meeting." Years ago
  when we were less disciplined, one of us would
  get a "hot tip" and run to the doorway of one of
  our partners, discuss it quickly and sometimes
  buy the stock. Now we are disciplined and use
  our monthly meeting as our forum. So, let's add
  to that: BUY CONSERVATIVE, QUALITY
  ONLY. We, at first, sprinkled 10–25% speculative stocks in our portfolio and growth potential
  stocks for half the balance. It simply did not
  work. During the recession of 1973–74 we were
  sadly made aware of an erosion of values. So we
  now buy 100% quality; *AND*

- We buy for yield. I somewhere earlier stated that
  the greatest invention in the world was compound interest. 5% per year compounded is
  great, 6% better and 10% will retire you quickly.
  With our dividend and interest yield, plus some
  growth, we've compounded 10 %. Stocks go up
  and down. But, if they come back to the original
  price, at least we (you) will have your 6% compound growth. Don't try to make a killing and
  you will get rich.

- Don't get wedded to any stock. We're married to
  our spouses and partners and anything else is
  saleable. Stock is a piece of paper. If it's made
  money or lost money, be willing to sell it if the
  experts tell you to do so. Our greatest losses were

from watching a stock drift down and down and down and hoping it would recover. Now we sell it if it goes down 20%. We also are disciplined to sell at a profit. My personal rule is to sell any Grade A stock at 50% profit. No one, including my partners or broker agrees. But, if you are buying good quality you're not likely to get a lot more than this percentage, so sell. More importantly, it's a discipline to *realize*, take your profit and go on the other more current possibilities for another 50%.

- Needless to say, diversify. We use and mix varying percentages of bonds, convertible bonds, preferred and common stocks. Our Pension Plan, being on a fixed formula basis and needing only 4% per year growth, is a little more conservative than our Profit Sharing Plan.

- Have one secretary make sure all dividends and bond interest are received. It sounds foolish, but we carry a total of about 30 separate issues in both plans. That's 30 securities paying dividends or interest two to four times a year. Even the best corporate trustee's or broker's computer may lose one or two a year. A simple chart check-off has given us in some years over $1,000 of "found money." This same secretary, properly trained, can easily handle (a) the monthly deposits, (b) dividend/interest check-off, (c) setting up the monthly meetings, (d) securing and distributing the monthly computer runout, and (e) drafting a yearly report to the participants. It takes her less than 2 hours a month to do all these things. But if she recovers even one "lost" dividend, isn't it worth it?

- Keep the employees informed of their interest and benefits. One of the purposes is to create an incentive for the experienced worker to stay on to make the group more money. Don't be secretive and hide from any employee the benefits accumulating.

I purposely haven't gone into details of the specifics of the plans or their administration. That's up to you and your advisors. The money you'll save will make it well worth the expenditure.

RULES:

1. *Start both a Profit Sharing Plan and Pension Plan.*

2. *Be conservative and disciplined in its operation and management.*

XIII
KEEPING RECORDS LIKE A BUSINESS
or
Why Not? It Is One!

I'm constantly amazed when visiting other law firms, large, medium and small, with their lack of systems and records. Some may have old systems useful for a single practitioner, but never refined or updated as the firm grew to 2, 4, 10 or 20 lawyers. Others have too few systems or none at all. This costs you money! You must realize that your office is a business; that poor records and systems drain money from you and your partner.

What type of systems and record keeping am I referring to that helps make money?*

---

*I can't even start to relate all of them so will discuss briefly the most obvious. Also, as I said in the Prologue, I'm not going to give you a specific form, rather, the reason for using one. I cannot in this limited book give you all reasons, justifications and benefits for use. But they are manyfold and any law library has volumes and loose leafs filled with a myriad of forms.

Incoming Business Memo. I referred to this in Chapter IX. It's a check against ultimately losing billing which represents the *net return* for your work product. Its advantages were earlier related in Chapter IX.

Procedure Manual. This was discussed in detail in Chapter VIII. The savings in time to both the newer employee asking questions and the older ones answering them has to be obvious. The uniformity of practice, accuracy and legal protections are bonuses!

Time Sheets. This has to be a must even for a contingent fee lawyer, who may have to justify his time at a later date. Some don't bother to keep any but rely on memory or "what the traffic will bear". Without time sheets you're living in an older world, and without doubt, frequently giving your clients an unintended free service.

Letter Copies. So what's the big deal? Doesn't everyone make yellow or Xerox copies of all letters, memos and transmittals for the file? We also make a pink and blue—and not just to have pretty colors around the office; it's not a color game. The *pinks* are gathered daily and passed from lawyer to lawyer; Each scans what the other did. There are several reasons; clients who phone one of several can't play one lawyer against another. Each lawyer, at least generally, knows the status of most matters by reviewing the "pinks". Also, if the writer has made a "blooper" the others might be able to tell him. Of course, in very large firms this couldn't be done by that method, but it could be done by departments or compartmentalized. It's another check and discipline.

The *blues* are the best follow-up system we've ever found. Every letter, memo, or request of mine has a blue copy, which comes *to me* after 10 days. I must *personally* review my own, 6 to 20 of them daily, to discard the ones already answered, or follow-up on those that need it, or mark ahead for 15 days or a month those that require no action then. The secretary cannot review them. It's mandatory I do it as it's my possible malpractice, my certificate and my reputation. It also expedites follow-ups. I can write a note on a blue and my secretary can then follow-up, but I initiate it. It's a time saver and time expeditor.

Master Case List. We have a master case list which compiles every case we have in the office. Its headings are:

Atty in Charge	Backup Atty	Client	Matter	Status

At a meeting every 4 to 6 weeks, the lawyers review the list, take off completed cases, add new ones, discuss those that require special handling, and shift cases for vacations or sabbaticals coming up. Attached to this is a list of all cases we've referred out of the office. We still have a duty to a client to monitor and follow-up, if necessary. This is our reminder.

Petty Cash. How much do you lose through carelessness or by partners and associates forgetting to put in chits? Well, we stopped this by making one person responsible *and accountable and no one else has a key to the fund.* It saved us roughly $100 a month, plus more accurate charges to the clients for part reimbursement where applicable.

Annual Corporate Minutes Follow-Up. We formerly handled annual minutes haphazardly when and if we got to them. We set up a systematic follow-up card system with one secretary in-charge (and with the format described in the Procedure Manual). It's done automatically monthly, when due. Clients Profit Sharing and Pension Plans minutes reflecting all contributions and. authorizations are also handled in exactly the same manner. At a very reasonable charge we picked up over $350 in a month with our system.

Safekeeping. Over a period of years we have found that some documents would be left in a file, or a drawer, or a safe, or whatever that particular lawyer in charge of the case thinks best. Now, any document of value goes in a bank safe deposit box, with a copy in the file, of course. They are all catalogued and indexed on cards by client, matter and date, *and it's kept current* as matters are placed in and taken out. Stock certificates, notes, escrow papers, marriage certificates, savings passbooks, assignments, various receipts, original letter or memo of intent, pink ownership slips, power of attorney, client's original deeds and insurance policies—We *know* where it is and we save money with the index by its use. The time we formerly used for a search is now saved and is billable on other work done.

Filing System Checklist. We follow the filing system of having (a) active, (b) transferred, and (c) dead files. The former two are on the premises and the latter at paid storage.* We have a master list and system for retrieval for both transferred and the dead files that is fast and sure. It's our time that costs money, so we try to save it for better things. If you've just let it grow because your chief secretary of 30 years likes it that way (and she knows where *she* can find things), you may be paying for a lot of sentimentality. If she retires or quits, you've got problems.

Budget and Periodic Financial Statements. You may feel that these are esoteric and reserved for the "big boys". Can I tell you that many of the "big boys" don't have them and it's costing them money—just as it's costing you money not to. Even if it's an approximate, loose budget you can start to determine, after 3 to 6 months, what items have gone awry and act accordingly to save on these. You can refine your preparation of the budgets each year and watch for leaks. The monthly or quarterly balance sheet and profit and loss

---

*It's not important which of the many filing systems you use as long as it is systematic, time saving and sure. But if it's helter-skelter and just grew like topsy then it's costing you money and should be revised.

statements will likewise tell you what you're doing. The cost is small; it's worth it.

New File Memo. Talk about saving money. Does the inside left cover side of every one of your files have a new file memo with pertinent information necessary to save your staff—and you—time? When you or your secretary have to phone the client, are the correct names and numbers there? Is the up-to-date address to write to there? Is the name, address and phone number of the opposing attorneys there? Does your bookkeeper have the address to send the bill? Is the exact name of the opposition party there? If we but realized the time spent on these many details; all to be saved by a simple initiatory memo kept in the file.

Of course, there are other forms we use that have been adapted to our practice. But every one originates with the thought of saving time—spelled M - O - N - E - Y. We use status memos, service parties lists, billing breakdown sheet (for major clients), and other forms, but use them we do.

You may say that with all the time spent on forms we leave less to practice law. Just the opposite. You spend an inordinate amount of time spinning your wheels in an unorganized manner. We each spend 5 minutes a day on our "blues", ten on our "pinks", 5 on our time sheets. We spend jointly an hour or so a month on our master case list; one of us spends 5 minutes a day on new business memo, and 15–30 minutes a month on our Budget and Financial Statement. The women spend a little time on the Procedure Manual, the annual minutes, new file memos, and safekeeping. But the overall savings from this is many hours, totaling days each month—all billable at $50-100 per hour. A fair trade, believe me.

RULE:

Be systematic; adopt good forms and use them to save time.

XIV
THE "PERSONAL"
CLIENT-LAWYER
RELATIONSHIP

or

Switching Cases And Clients Is Good For all

Here, dear reader, I'm afraid I'll lose you if I haven't already done so. Try switching cases *and* clients with various other lawyers in the office, both partners and associates. Where I've tried to teach you to tighten up on your techniques and systems to make more money, you might go part way, but when I tell you to give your clients to your partners (and vice versa), and let them try your cases (and vice versa), you'll rebel because now your ego will be bruised.

You can't believe another can do it as well as you!

You can't believe your client will put up with another lawyer!

Wrong on both scores; and that error is, costing you money, leisure and ease of practice. How often have you really felt you couldn't take your four-week vacation a year because your favorite client is going into a big deal? Big Deal!! How often have you handled a divorce or personal type matter because your next-best client felt more comfortable with you than anyone else in the office? Have you ever wanted to take a scholastic course, run away for a week and do something foolish or play two days of golf mid-week instead of always on a weekend? But you feel you can't. You probably personally do many jobs that are better suited to a younger associate because of your underlying fear of losing contact with your personal clients.

I can bet that most of the firms of two or more lawyers are really small fiefdoms of individual practices just joined together for convenience. There may be some helping one another, but each has his favorite and close clients.

We've developed a philosophy that the clients are office clients *and not that of any individual lawyer.* They don't hire Bert Silver or Marty Rosen, but Silver, Rosen, Fischer & Stecher. They know—or soon learn—that any case brought in will be handled from the inception by a lawyer whose experience and longevity of practice is equal to that case; and will hopefully accomplish the best result at the lowest cost to the client.

The first time a new client comes in he may specify one particular lawyer, and it's likely we will accomodate him. But, he's soon made aware of our overall system and philosophy and told the reasons for it.

Further, any pending case may be switched from one lawyer to another comparably experienced. This also is part of our ideology. Such substitution can happen when a vacation, sabbatical or trial conflict occurs; or a large case comes into the office; or one lawyer becomes ill. Remember I mentioned in Chapter X about speed and the profitability of expediting and finishing cases? If we postponed matters and didn't exchange cases, the clients' results are delayed and we make less money. By exchanging cases when necessary or feasible we expedite them and make MORE money.

You also remember I talked of a uniform filing system and it being in order and up-to-date. One of the reasons for this is that each lawyer and secretary can readily and expeditiously get into the new case. The new lawyer taking it over is apt initially to use the former lawyer's secretary because of her familiarity with the case.

We've never, to our knowledge, lost a client because of the implementation of the two principles stated above. We've only had three clients in 16 years refuse to work with a particular lawyer because of personality conflict, but, all three are still clients and work with any and all others. Thus, we recognize that there may be personality conflicts and are willing to work around them. If that same client continues to find fault with the next lawyer assigned to his matter, and then the next one, it simply means he wants all matters handled by one particular person. That we cannot and will not do. They retain the firm, not one specific professional.

Now you can see why we so carefully pick our partners and associates; so they can work in and fit in the total picture.

The philosophy of switching clients and cases must be constantly asserted and practiced. We know there's a tendency to assuage one's ego and to feel indispensible in the eyes of a favorite client, who we've nurtured and helped build. There's a tendency to downplay competitors, even our own partners. We do just the opposite in order to foster and encourage this supplantation idea. It means more money to each of us, time off and better service to the customer, so we constantly struggle against divisiveness and fractionalization of effort or client.

Believe it or not, it has had two beneficial tangential consequences. The partner becomes *more* indispensible to the firm (rather than the client) and there is less struggle to get "my" client attached to "me." We found that the result was a more cohesive and cooperative team.

Can you try to accept these two concepts of switching clients and cases? Can you picture the flexibility of being able to and the resulting benefits and economies? Perhaps you can now start to see that the precepts you read about above are not ethereal, but practical and start to tie together. When we said we upgrade cases and clients by dropping out bad ones and poor paying ones, it gave us the time and ability to allow exchange of those we do handle from a more active, busy lawyer, at that moment, to one less occupied. Now perhaps, you may understand why each of our lawyers can, and do, take one month off (and I've taken two months or more) every year. They know that their cases will be handled, just as they will handle other's cases when the other is gone. Also, since no client belongs to them personally, the client accepts the idea of talking to another lawyer when vacation, illness or being out-of-town creates an empty office, another reason for partnership versus sole practitioner.

You can turn this concept into a big plus in the client's eyes, right from the beginning. I'm sure you've had a client telephone to give or receive information when you're gone. He's miffed. Who does he talk to? He may not know others in the office. Well, we handle it differently. We normally have another partner or associate (at no extra cost to the client) sit in from the first—particularly if he's going to do the inside work on it. I tell the client that he's sitting in so that somebody else will know what's going on if I'm out of the office; that the matter won't stop. *We tell* the client we want another lawyer to know what's going on. Why not tell him? It's the truth. You'd be surprised; the client likes it. He now has two lawyers he can phone; you've broken him into your interchange concept; you've raised the stature of "junior" to an associate; you've made your firm more money by releasing you for more hours of higher paying work.

Why shouldn't you switch and exchange cases? If you go on trial for a week or month should all of your other business stop? Isn't that unfair to other clients who are forced into this delay? The partial alternative is to work double at the office, on weekends and nights, a quick phone call at meals, to keep a practice going. But we don't work Saturdays or Sundays or nights and we still get our work done by substituting for one another.

You may be a sketpic and a disbeliever, but it works and is truly a more modern method of doing business.

RULES:

1. Learn to switch cases with your other lawyers.

2. Learn to switch clients with your other lawyers.

XV

THE ORGANIZED FIRM

or

Meetings and Statistics Only Confuse Me

Hopefully this book will give you not just ideas to make your practice more profitable, but it will make it easier for you. Meetings are one method of doing this if they don't become ritualistic.

I hate meetings and the interminable speeches that generally add up to little.

So our organized meetings are different. Let me show why and how our efficiency is maximized.

We all meet for 10 minutes first thing every Tuesday morning. When I say all, I mean lawyers, secretaries, receptionist* and clerk. We find out who has crunches, who needs

---

*Yes, the phone does get answered. It's handled by the receptionist who quietly takes all messages so the calls can be returned immediately after the meeting.

help, who can help and what big jobs or deadlines are coming up that week. If we have to switch cases or loads, this is a
good time to find out about it. If one lawyer is on trial or
vacation, you'd be surprised how often at our office his
secretary volunteers and says, "Mr. Stecher gave me about
three days work, I can help you after tomorrow!" We may
realize our library or files need extra work, and so we hire a
temporary clerk or secretary. The meetings have an auxil-
iary benefit; they make each employee an active participant
who then tries to pitch in and help. The fiefdoms and divisiveness tends to disappear. That's worth untold
money—and expedited work.

Another meeting is that of the lawyers who meet monthly
to go over their master case list, and do their billing. It can't
be boring as it moves too fast. I've already described the
billing sessions (Chapter IX) and the safeguards used to
pick up money every month that many of you lose. Either
before or after is a review of the master case list (Chapter
XIII). It's at that session that most exchange of cases are
accomplished. It's here that *possible or contingent* case sub-
stitutions are noted. John may expect to be called out on
trial just when he's going to be on vacation, so Mike or
Marty might have to handle the matter. Or, if two hearings
are set on one day and if one doesn't abort, then Marty
might give one to Bert or John. When I talked about not
asking for postponements, I meant it. Unless absolutely
mandatory for the client's benefit (not ours), we proceed; so
our meeting is partly for this purpose. The other ac-
complishment is bringing the master calendar to date—
dropping off completed matters and adding new ones.

We also meet once a month, usually a little before and
then during lunch, for review of our Profit Sharing and
Pension Plans. Our analyst-broker is there, and we review
our two portfolios, talk long range, short range, sometimes
buy, sometimes sell and sometimes do nothing. We don't do
all those things every month; what we do depends on condi-

tions, but it's a discipline that has made us a considerable amount of money since we started. I say "made us" because just putting it away is more than most lawyers do. Our meetings means dollars to us.

Our last meeting is a yearly shareholder's or partner's one. I know most very large firms have them in one form or another, most small firms don't. *The purpose is to plan long range policy and implement new ideas.* Any discussion of pending cases is taboo. We have an agenda that's been building from the prior year and may be added to at the meeting. We have the notes of the last year's meetings in order to determine if what we decided then was accomplished. We do not meet in the office, but in a motel meeting room or an apartment that's purposely deserted for the day. We start early in the morning, have lunch there (cold cuts and beer), and adjourn temporarily for dinner. We break up when we are done, usually 10 or 11 in the evening. It's a great opportunity to discuss all types of matters. Some in the past have included:

- Salary review and levels
- New typewriter systems
- New space requirements
- How big should the firm grow
- Satisfaction of personnel
- Sabbatical duration and years due
- Increase in Pension benefits
- New fee levels
- Bringing in new partners
- Altering our type of practice
- Upgrading and client selection
- Divisiveness and fractionalization
- Our own building
- New systems and record keeping
- Reviewing old systems

- Incorporation vs. partnership
- Computerization for research and other phases

I certainly recognize that many lawyers and firms talk of some or even all of these matters, but doing it at lunch or in the office or over drinks with less than all partners there creates problems and insufficiencies. Hence, our yearly meeting all together in privacy.

One more thought on meetings. The time they take is more than made up by the economies affected, efficiencies innovated, money recovered and new long-range ideas developed.

We have an office manager as all small firms should. Someone has to direct the traffic and make sure we function with supplies, telephones, screen personnel for hiring, keep personnel records, schedule vacations and the numerous details that require *constant* overseeing. The office manager may be a lawyer or a top executive secretary. You just can't pick anyone, or rotate it. Three important qualities are needed: impartiality, objectivity and administrative ability. The receptionist should be under the direct supervision of the office manager since she does much of the detail concerning supplies, petty cash, form files, safe deposit, calendaring and the like. The office manager may also be responsible to supervise the interchange and flow of work to the secretaries.

Two other reviews should be mentioned, each of which saves actual cash each year.

One partner or associate is in charge of the library and periodicals and is responsible for *a yearly review of all renewals*. I've constantly been astounded at the lackadaisical continuance of incoming books, pocket parts and periodicals in firms of all sizes. There is little control or attempt to cut off those that are duplicative, outdated or not read. So someone is directly charged with this task. We saved about $1,100 the first year we did this. Review each year catches a few more items that were once worthwhile but now have little current value in view of our changing practice or different business emphasis.

One partner is in charge of a review of our budget. What good does that do? Have you an accurate idea of the build-up of dues and memberships a lawyer can accumulate? We looked it over and were able to eliminate some and save money. Contributions are controlled by prior decisions, not just allowed to grow like topsy. When a secretary says to her direct boss that she needs something, she isn't told, "Go get it". We are a generous firm and believe in modern equipment to please our personnel, but there has to be some control. We've even found ourselves buying rolodexes, paper holders, sorters and the like, only to find that in our storeroom we have many—some almost new.

Even our banking is organized. We have the usual type accounts for general business, trust and savings. But we have a reserve account which we use periodically for special purposes:

(a) We deposit monthly, exactly like rent, our pro rata estimated Profit Sharing Plan and Pension Plan contribution.

(b) If we expect heavy capital expenditures we do likewise.

(c) Estimated corporate income or gross receipts taxes are set aside.

(d) If we feel that our gross and net will suffer from a partner's sabbatical leave, we put away a reserve in advance to cover this expense.

We use this reserve account specifically to make sure we won't abandon any of these concepts from either lack of money or being pressed for available cash. Each function is viable and feasible; but without preparing for them there would be a temptation to abandon or defer one or more. Hence, just like rent, we set aside enough money monthly to cover our commitments.

Every step we've taken in making ourselves business-like, organized and functional have been taken with a view to making us more profitable. This is important if we intend to live well off the fruits of our legal work. Not so strangely, every one of our meetings and supervisory chores has given us, in the overall picture, more efficient time to actually practice law; they have also cut out unnecessary expenses. Both result in money in your pocket.

RULES:

1. Control your practice; don't let it control you.

2. Meetings of personnel will help your efficiency, but be brief and to the point.

XVI
OBTAINING NEW CLIENTS
or
Now You Can Advertise

If we're busy, why do we want more new business? We want to upgrade and keep new blood flowing into the practice. How do we get more business to fill in the spare time we've created from the many efficiencies?

So far we haven't advertised in our local papers and magazines, but we've developed methods of serving old and new clients to satisfy their needs. In doing so, we've affirmatively sought new *good* business within the bounds of ethical standards.

Many of our brethren believe that simply producing a workmanlike product and laboring hard for the client helps bring in new business. We do too, but we feel more is required. We don't want drones for associates or partners; we don't want some partners primarily for business-getting purposes and others primarily for production. We look ahead to retirement of the older partners and moving up of the younger. We want all of our partners and associates to participate in business acquisition, which is done in many ways. These methods may seem very obvious, but, honestly ask yourself if you really follow some, most, all, or none of them. To us they are part of the overall practice and just as important as office or trial work. They are acts of public relations.

Each of us from time to time writes articles after thorough research. Obviously, as specialists, they are usually in our own field, but a generalist can do the same using as a starting point a novel point of law from a memo or appellate brief. *And send or give your clients and potential clients a copy of it.* The publication of your name raises your stature to the public and other lawyers and has a distinctive meaning.

We encourage giving talks on frequent occasions to various groups for the same purpose, both in and out of any speciality we may have, but here it can be expanded to fraternal, social, neighborhood, church, womens', stock, investment or business groups. Sounds foolish and self-seeking, but particularly as a young lawyer, often many potential clients are impressed; if they are also young, they will grow in stature with you.

Participation in various civic, church, industry and trade groups brings business. The attendant participation and a willingness to become active enriches a social life, helps community activity and also brings business. Trite and tiresome, you might say, but most successful lawyers have done this.

Activity and attendance at some conventions and trade luncheons and dinners are fertile fields of new business. If you're a general practitioner or a specialist, you can become known at State Bar Conventions and get good referral business from other lawyers looking for your type of service. You will also meet some to whom you'll turn. If you're a very limited specialist you can be a part of a trade convention in your industry, which your clients attend. You can participate, feel at home and meet many more potential clients in that industry. It's a natural. You'll be called on to express your legal views—do so. Broadcasting, retailing, communications, trucking, warehousemen, construction, law enforcement, restaurants, and travel agents, just to name a few industries and fields, are great possibilities for convention attendance. I might also point out that we insist the married lawyer's wife attend with him, if at all possible—for several reasons. If the client wants to talk business or industry matters and his wife is along, it is not awkward. Also, by your wife's participation, note taking, client follow-up, and attendance at functions, her trip becomes business oriented and deductible.

Some lawyers deal in fields where some matters require joint participation by several, or many, in that area, some of whom are clients. Acceptance of such representation may result in your clients bringing in others similarly situated, who are also potential clients. Representation of a trade association gets your name in front of all members. It expands your possibility of choices.

The simple use of the mails is an excellent means of keeping in touch with clients, friends and potential clients. Every announcement we receive from another lawyer, doctor, accountant, birth of a child, marriage, or other event, elicits a personal letter from us. Whether they are forms on an automatic typewriter or handled by your secretary is unimportant. If the sender mails 100, 200 or 500 announcements, and receives back 2 or 3 congratulatory responses, he's going to damn well remember the responders, and he may, incidentally, have a good case someday. When you read in the paper of a promotion of a friend or someone does something nice for you, do not ignore these events or wait until you see the person; we constantly are dispatching thank you, sympathy and congratulatory notes right then, and people remember. Every time we get a case from anyone, whether it be another client, a friend, another lawyer, a stranger or anyone at all, we feel he or she is entitled to a note of gratitude. Do you realize how few do this? The effect is startling!

On the same view, we frequently give gifts. We have no referral fees and never have; we split no fees. Our gifts are not necessarily of great value. If we are highly recommended by someone and he's a wine buff, we may send him a bottle or a case of wine. He'll never forget us. If he and his wife are going on a cruise, we arrange to send a card and a bottle of champagne to their table on one of their nights at sea. The effect is salutory! If we see a client or someone who is a booster of ours at a restaurant, we send a round of drinks or a bottle of wine. As my wife has said of many phases of life, "Bread cast upon the waters comes back buttered." *DON'T BE CHEAP!*

Of course, we use the traditional method of keeping our name in front of clients and friends by Christmas cards and announcements of additions to our firm or change in location, but we do it so it benefits others or has a novel twist to it. For example, instead of sending a usual fancy Christmas card that gets lost in the shuffle, we make a donation to a charity in the name of each client, and they receive an inexpensive, plainly printed card announcing the donation. The charity reaps a benefit; the client or potential client feels far better—and they remember us. On an office announcement, we may superimpose a caricature of our new building or a truck or bus showing our specialty. It works.

The average lawyer misses so many opportunites to reach potential clients. How often have you tried a case, used a witness (doctor, merchant, laborer, or anyone), let him get off the stand and forgotten about him or her completely? Why not have your secretary send each a personal letter of thanks for their time and effort? Can you imagine their feeling on receiving it? We've done this for every witness we've used; the follow-up client acquisition even years later, is startling. It gets additional business.

If you deal with a public agency or trade association with any frequency, you get to know their personnel, particularly if you are constantly filing documents with one or several offices. Have you any idea how they feel about your office staff or lawyers? Or don't you care? Visit them occasionally and in a fair, open approach, find out if there are any irritations or gripes. Some goodwill may clear up possible gripes, and it may even get you referrals of good business.

Most of the above ideas are longer range and intangible, but there are several things that can be done at any time directly with clients. Frequently we lawyers put off getting new business because we are so busy. With the free time you are getting by upgrading and expediting you can now handle new business. How? Easy! *First,* discuss with your clients new subject matters that particularly apply to him where legal work is required or beneficial: A new will, an incorporation he once mentioned to you, a possible sale of a business, or taking his son in as a partner. Instead of always *reacting* to his initiatory ideas, why not practice "preventative law" and give him some ideas. That you might, incidentally, get some good new business is fine, but you're also doing him a real and true service. *Second,* make it a practice to keep your clients, or a particular type or group, informed of changes in the law that might particularly affect them. The new estate and gift tax rules mean possible changes in every will or *inter vivos* trust in your office. When this passed did you go through your will files and advise clients of the changes? ERISA and Keogh liberalization had an impact on retirement concepts. Did you let clients know of their impact? A new corporate law might mean new action by every closely held or family corporation. A proposed rezoning ordinance might require many of your property holding clients to take some immediate action. A proposed or new state property tax relief might help or hurt your clients. Most lawyers do nothing but wait for their "customers" to phone or write. Why not do a favor for each group, class or industry type of client and write each a similar letter advising him of the action that has or might personally affect him. If it were not for this action on your part they may never know about it, or if they do, they might do nothing from inertia or procrastination. A straight-forward letter may satisfy your duty to them and often also develops worthwhile business.

A new young lawyer can certainly use this last means of advertising his "availability." He can write to friends and family about newly enacted laws on taxes, testamentary disposition or similar subjects. The tenor can be "I know I don't represent you but thought you might not know that . . . ." The recipients may likely already have a lawyer. But the recipient may (a) want to spread his business, or (b) be grateful for the information being called to his attention. It brings new business for new lawyers.

In reviewing the few ideas above that encompass methods of securing new immediate and long-range business, there's none that in any way violate any canon of ethics. Several satisfy a duty a lawyer has to his client. Most show a willingness to make the lawyer available to his client. If open and blatant advertising is acceptable today, why not these more subtle methods?

RULES:

1. Upgrade by developing new business.

2. Plan long-range methods to do it.

3. Activate immediate methods to do it.

XVII
ECONOMY AND EFFICIENCY
or
It's Worth A Try To Save Money

Government employment just grows. There's little attempt to control it by thoughtful means. Cities, states and
Federal governments start worthwhile projects and employ
workers, but even when the need ceases or diminishes, the
project continues.

That's similar to Parkinson's Law. Lawyers and law firms
usually follow the same principle, only to a lesser extent.

If you were to review your operation, I'd conservatively
estimate you could save from $500 per year to $10,000 by
eliminating expenses for unnecessary supplies, periodicals,
contributions, dues and equipment. In Chapter XV, I mentioned the benefit of developing and maintaining a budget.
It's a prod to economizing, but even if you don't (or won't)
have a budget, you can still save money. Let's explore just
four simple areas.

First, list every item of *dues* you've built up over a period of years. Go through your books, checkbook or membership cards. You'll find almost every one worthwhile, but some passé or not attended and used. I won't single out any specific names, but we were astounded to find in one review nine (9) organizations, the membership of which we could dispose. We had joined because we were interested in it at that time, or a friend asked us to or . . . ??? So we saved $285 per year on this one item alone. The worse part was that some of the memberships were carried without our ever really knowing definitely we were still paying for them. My secretary would get the dues notice, recognize I had been a member for 16 years and approve it for payment. The review was enlightening—and the savings more profitable to us.

Then we reviewed our *periodicals,* supplements and pocket parts. Like many lawyers we try to pretend we're knowledgeable and keep up on current laws. When the boycott and energy crunch came in 1973, we were innundated with new rules on fuel allocations, conservation and pricing, so we ordered a loose-leaf service. Another time we did the same when Price and Wage Control was ordered under Phases I through XVI. We used to form and administer Profit Sharing and Pension Plans for clients, so we had some books on this subject and the inevitable annual pocket parts. Our tax services grew to that of about two-thirds the size of a specialist, yet we had cut down our tax work and frequently used outside counsel. One day we had a list prepared of every service, pocket part, set and periodical we were receiving and the cost thereof. It was amazing that without any disagreement we cut out seven unnecessary items (totaling $415 per year) and, with some compromise, agreed to terminate another four ($525 per year). We were not only that much richer, but:

- our woman in charge of the library saved time and effort

- we saved time by not circulating the periodicals and topical front sheets

- we made more workable room in our always expanding library.

Now, review of these expenditures is done annually to prevent another build-up.

Another fertile area of some economy is regulating of *yearly contributions.* Perhaps you make NONE, so you don't have this problem. We did! It grew like topsy: a church "souvenir journal," a twenty-fifth year bulletin, The Community Fund or Policeman's Ball. It got haphazard and unmanageable. A partner gave to his favorite and turned down others more worthy. So again, we had the bookkeeper make a list of a full year's past contributions, and it verified our bad handling. Now we budget an amount we feel is generous, but maximum. We instituted a simple system of priorities and agreements—a small savings, but efficient.

I'll give one last example of economies in mentioning the buying of *office supplies.* My review of other offices' procedures indicates that this is one of the largest "drains" in the system. In the early days you bought from the nearest stationery store or supply house and from one of the nice guys who peddled out of his catalogue. So, it was only a small loss because you didn't buy a lot per month after the initial opening order of everything, but then your office grew in (a) size and, (b) possibly also, number of lawyers. Yet, you still buy haphazardly, except your secretary does it. Worse yet, each secretary does it. Worse yet, everybody does it. You can be certain you're paying far too much for the necessary items. We fell into that trap until one of our younger lawyers and his secretary very easily compared what we were then paying for our paper, yellow tablets, foolscap, ballpoints, scotch tape, ribbons and facial tissues, to a more realistic cost if we bought all or most from a better source.

We saved approximately 16% of $22,600 per year, or $4,972. That's a worthy sum to play around with. It's a sum that each succeding year is saved and helps pay for the contributions to our Plans.

I've described four methods of economies above, each of which has worked for us, and will work for you. There are other fields we attacked and saved: limiting client's advances saved losses and interest on capital, uniformity of equipment cut down on odd-ball items that were unused when a secretary quit, recapture of long distance telephone calls and telegrams brought more harvest of savings. There are many areas to look at.

Throughout I've talked and stressed efficiencies. We try to practice its application because it makes us money. So to the greatest extent possible, we attempt uniformity of equipment and systems. We're each individuals and like ingenuity and individualistic style, but we sublimate some of these traits to gain uniformity in certain areas. We buy the same typewriters. We formerly found that each secretary had a separate preference in make and type, but when she terminated, we had a difficult time satisfying her successor. Finally we went to the use of all the same model typewriters. Besides having only one serviceman (a saving of our time) we can interchange documents or sheets, between various typists and expedite the work output. There's uniformity of type and set-up of letters that impresses an observant client; no longer does he get a letter with gothic type from one and pica from another. The uniformity allows our lawyers to interchange cases without awkwardness.

Our answer to dictating machines are the same. We haven't locked ourself in with one transcriber working with only one man's product. If one secretary is sick or on vacation, the work still flows. The lawyer may have preferred a different product, but is willing to use the same as others for the many reciprocal benefits.

Our paper is uniform, as are our ribbons. We no longer cater to each secretary as to what she prefers. If we can bend and adjust in our use of dictating equipment, she can on the use of a typewriter and paper. No longer do we have one type of bond for one woman and a different type for another. No longer do we have different erasers and removers. By this means, several women can work on various parts of the same documents at the same time.

We've simply found that a uniformity of supplies is efficient and money/time saving. We practice it and except for an initial shock, the secretaries accept and like it. In our storage room we still have tangible evidence of past purchased equipment used by former secretaries who had idiosyncratic tastes. We have five different typewriter paper holders, four telephone recall systems, two odd-paper sorters, six different foot transcribers, two unusable ear pieces, five unmatched desk calendar stands,. . . . I could go on and on but I stopped listing the junk from disgust. It represents money lost and stands as a simple memorial to it not being repeated.

We resisted the buying of an automatic typewriter until we finally realized we were falling into the idea, "We didn't need it up to now, why start?" We investigated and counted up its assets. We started with one and stayed there. One secretary uses it and is most proficient. But remember we exchange work, so it was possible to channel her the work that was re-do and repetitious, and best used her good skills and the machine's attributes. We probably will purchase another one, as we have found that there's a noticeable saving of time/money, as well as a better work product.

I've noted earlier other methods we used to encourage proficient work. Short form letters, handwritten replies on an incoming letter, workable and expedited follow-up system, upgrading clients and cases, short meetings, joint billing, and so many more. I was tempted to say "none alone are great money savers, but in the aggregate. . . .," but I'd be wrong. Each are time and money savers that alone are worth innovating. In the aggregate, their use will increase your profit enough to make a full contribution to your Profit Sharing and Pension Plans. That's a bold statement, but true. It's worked for us.

RULES:

1. *Economize by periodic review of various categories of expenses such as periodicals, contributions, supplies and dues.*

2. *Efficiencies through uniformity of equipment, concentration of purchasing and other systems will make you money.*

XVIII
A HAPPY OFFICE PAYS
DIVIDENDS
or
It Takes More Than Just Tickling

By now I'm sure you think I'm a dreamer. The ideas of no procrastination, budgets, exchanging cases, joint billing sounds ridiculous to the average lawyer or firm. It has only the benefit of making gobs of money.

So let met give you another "novel" idea. Purposely run a happy office!

I know that sounds so obvious. But is it? Ever listen to your secretaries lament and bitch? Ever hear them sound off?

We found years ago that productivity was in direct proportion to the staff's satisfaction with surrounding working conditions, and productivity means money.

Two people more than any other, were responsible for this perception. My long-time partner Marty, and an angel of a secretary, Jean. Let me relate what each showed me and then tie them together.

Marty instituted generosities and liberalisms in benefits to all employees, some of which I've described earlier. I already mentioned that we pay higher secretarial and associates' salaries than comparable firms in our area. Other top qualified secretaries who've heard of our system want to work for us so we get the pick of the field. We've actually heard from many of them how hard our secretaries voluntarily work to prove their worth and earn what they get. Then, if we add the generous Profit Sharing and Pension Plan allocations, you can understand the significance of it. They're willing and want to produce more, to be paid more in order to get 25% more in contributions; and by their hard work we owners profit.

It just isn't dollars paid and contributed but also liberality of rules. In our Plans we have only a six month wait for a new employee to participate and thereafter a 20% per year vesting rule. It's not a shadowy future benefit, but almost an immediate one that they can taste, touch, feel and see. The effect on their morale is startling!

We talked generosity. We have practiced it in our insurance plans. Remember, we personally are covered also, so we benefit from the fringes! Besides the required workers compensation and state disability, we carry group policies.

- Life Insurance based on salary scale, but generally running $10,000–$15,000; and

- Basic Medical that covers usual hospitalization benefits, plus a major medical; and

- A Catastrophic Medical plan with a $250,000 limit; and

- A salary continuation plan which pays during
  full disability, 50% of salary for up to 5 years.

My partner's idea in liberal benefits was two-fold: to make
all our employees more willing *to work at our place,* and to
give them a sense of well-being while working there. It
works and has succeeded with tangible results. While we
don't like overtime nights or weekends, our secretaries and
associates frequently offer to work to get things out. When
we refuse, except for a real emergency, they work more
deligently during regular hours to produce. They help one
another. They help screen new personnel for better qualified workers to work with. And, they help train the new
people.

Thus they make us and themselves more profit.

Jean taught me something different. She really espoused
Emerson's doctrine that one "doesn't live by bread alone."
And she did it slowly, undiscerningly at first, but purposely.
At first she had a small cake and champagne for whoever
had a birthday. She set it for 5:00 p.m. (closing time) and we
all sat around the library table. The social exchange between all and the (at first restrained) celebration of the
birthday was obvious. It went well. After a few times it
became an office tradition with the firm paying the minor
cost and it being moved to 4:30 p.m. Everything stopped at
that time and we had 45 minutes to an hour of enjoyable
association. Strangely enough in the relaxed ambiance,
good business ideas were discussed and thought of.

One day Jean asked if just once we could have an office
dinner after our occasional quarterly business meeting. So
we did. Again, the drinks and sociability led to ideas, questions, suggestions and thoughts being presented that hadn't
been put forth in earlier office meetings. Some were good,
some humorous and discarded, but the sociability was

pleasant. So we made the dinner a once a year, or more often, event with spouses. Somehow it showed a new dimension to the personality of our co-workers.

We aren't a drinking office, nor do we adjourn to the bar after work, but once in a while someone would have a problem, personal or office, and my "spy" Jean would suggest I invite him or her for a drink after work. At first I rebelled feeling I could do it over the desk. But Jean was smarter and her approach better, so each of us follows this pattern on occasions—with salutory benefits. It's part of a personal equation that an employee respects and to which he or she reacts favorably.

We run generally, a formal but friendly office. In eight years Jean still called the lawyers "Mr." or "Ms.", but her friendliness and understanding led the tone to a friendly and understanding office.

Both the tangible and intangible benefits have been inculcated into our system. They pay off!!

RULES:

1. Be generous in benefits to the employees.

2. A friendly office will repay such benefits.

XIX
CONTINUING LAW EDUCATION
or
At Fifty I Can Still Learn– But Will I?

This is a short, vital, succinct chapter.

First: despite all the talk that "this is a movement whose time has come", when was the last time you took a CLE/ CEB* course to up-date your experienced but perhaps out-dated views? Do you treat recertification as a joke, or worse, as though that it applies to others but not you?

Second: Forgetting the courses on law subjects themselves, have you taken even one on fees, office procedures or office management? Have you done more in the past years than cursorily read an article in some lawyers' magazine?

The propensity of lawyers to refuse to re-educate themselves is appalling. Because we've handled probates and

---

*Some states or groups call the program "Continuing Education of the Bar)" (CEB); some call them "Continuing Legal Education" (CLE). I don't care what you call them as long as you use them.

corporations for years, we feel we are updated and "experts", but most are truly not. To make money in law necessitates an up-to-date periodic, if not constant, review of new procedures and laws. The ability to be able to phone a client and update him on revised statutes or new concepts implies a modern up-to-date view, *not* an aging hack. Yet, how many CLE/CEB courses have you taken on substantive, basic subjects?

If you're a doctor and don't keep up on advanced techniques, it's a life. In law it's a lost case or money.

If you don't keep up on substantive and procedural innovations, it's an almost sure bet you don't even bother to keep up on fees, office procedures or management. Yet, as earlier stated, that's where the money lies. Still, few lawyers bother to pursue any such subject in book or course form.

One of our partners recently presented a paper on office procedure, office manuals and billing practice to our specialized association. He listed seven pages of over 60 books and articles covering publications on every phase of the economics of law practice. They covered fees, management, library, pension plans, forms, equipment and systems, among other subjects, but in discussing the field with various lawyers, I've found few who have even bothered to read even one of these books. You must! Without others' ideas you're sterile and will stagnate. You can be the best legal scholar in the city or state, but that doesn't make you the best businessman. Others have ideas that you've never thought about; or if you've thought about them, never knew how to profitably implement them. These publications can help you.

Lastly, how many courses or single lectures have you attended in the past years on this subject? Every state or area has had some organized CLE/CEB or business oriented lawyer give one or more lectures on a subject that could make you money. It may be on fees, getting clients, Xerox use or even use of forms. It may be given by the Bar Association through CLE/CEB or a Barrister's Club; it may be by a business form or equipment company trying to get you to use its product. Ninety percent of the 2–3 hours may be wasted and boring. We've felt that *if we can get just one usable idea* from any lecture, course or book, it will more than make up for our time and ennui; *just one idea.* At least 35–40% of the ideas we've instituted that have made us money have come from this method—*just one idea* from a lecture course or book.

We don't limit participation to an office manager or managing partner. If he alone brings in the idea it becomes too limiting. We want all members to keep up-to-date, suggest changes and innovate ideas they have picked up. It makes more of them aware of the methods needed to increase profitability. That's our overall aim.

This book is intended to explain and demonstrate specific techniques and systems that have made more money for us in the law office. But the use of basic sound business principles of running an efficient firm are a preliminary step and a minimum requirement. In Chapter XIII I touched upon some few efficiencies in keeping records that will assist you. But you must take full advantage of all systems and procedures designed to help you on a day to day basis.

Besides the numerous books and articles on the subject there are consulting services that are expert in the field of legal economics and management practices.

Using a consulting company is not an admission of failure. There's a tendency in some cases not to use such a readily helpful tool because of such false connotation.

The lawyers in this country may not realize how very fortunate they are to have several private firms that give seminars, courses, lectures, forums and conferences in the business field dedicated to the furtherance of more proficient law offices. These companies are specialists.

The studies that some have made for various firms cover a myriad of business subjects, some of which have to be of interest to any law office that seeks to maximize its profit and/or make itself more efficient. A few of these many studies (for example only) were recently enumerated by Daniel J. Cantor & Company, Inc., one of the leaders in this field:

- "Complete Management Audit
- Organization Studies
- Future Planning
- Analysis of Income and Overhead
- Fees and Billing Policies
- Income Distribution Plans
- Associate Career Development
- Acquisition or Merger of Practices
- Administrative Systems and Financial Controls
- Feasibility of Computer and Automation
- Filing and Information Retrieval
- Relocation of Offices and Layout Plans
- Recruitment of Professional Administrators
- Retirement and Withdrawal Policies"

> *"Profitable Management for the Law Firm"*
> Number 2; Spring 1978
> Daniel J. Cantor and Company, Inc.

An "in-house" management study on an objective detached basis has to give some new ideas to a firm that will improve its workability and profitability.

Give serious thought to taking advantage of the services of an outside available company by (a) taking one or more of their courses or seminars and/or (b) an independent consultation. Whichever expert you may use (and there are several good ones), whichever forum or seminar you may attend or whichever lecture you listen to, you will have to get one (or more) new idea that will more than pay for the minimal expense and time involved.

Just One New Idea.

RULES:

1. *Substantive and procedural law is constantly changing. All must keep up.*

2. *Office management is equally as important and the lawyer must be kept current.*

3. *One good idea from a lecture, course or book repays the time and cost spent.*

XX
VACATIONS AND SABBATICALS
or
Your Ego Gets Bruised
When They Don't Miss You

Let's talk about a favorite subject—TIME OFF!

Lawyer's work is demanding and often performed under strict deadlines and great pressures which cumulatively affect his durability. You may think of yourself as superman but you are not. The lawyers' energies and physical resources are finite, have a limited life and are subject to rapid depletion. A prize fighter in round eight or a lawyer ready to submit a case to a jury MUST continue to the conclusion of that contest; but beyond that, he must later restore himself with a meaningful pause.

In our office we believe in investing in each lawyer that pause which is necessary to allow him to produce most effectively and most profitably for the longest period. Together with the other rules we've adopted we've found that substantial time off has several beneficial results:

- It's an investment in the physical, mental and spiritual well-being of the lawyer; by its use he will contribute both more valuable and more extended service to the law firm.

- It is a method of furthering and accomplishing the overall plan of the office to exchange clients and cases. By such time off the recipient and the others learn from practical experience it does work.

To accomplish these objectives, we have formulated three almost inflexible rules:

1. There shall be no night, Saturday or Sunday work except when on trial or in a real emergency; and,

2. Every partner, young or old, gets at least one-month vacation yearly, usually more in the case of the seniors; and,

3. Every five years on a rotating seniority basis the longer-time partners must take six months sabbatical with pay; the younger, new partners take three months, also with pay.

Your first reaction will be, "I wish we could!" Then you'll hark back to all the excuses as to why such a three-point plan won't work, but it does work if you'll let it. Our cardinal practice is to devise ways to make a good plan work, not conjure up reasons it won't work. Before briefly exploring the reasons and feasibility of the three rules above, please re-read or review Chapter XIV on switching cases and clients and relate it with the time off we take.

Five day a week schedule. If you're earning $25,000, $40,000 or $60,000 a year, but working late each night and either Saturday or Sunday, you're probably putting in 52 to 58 hours of work per week. Not only are you a workaholic but you are kidding yourself on your "earnings". Earnings are based on a reasonable work week; you are really making about $18,000 instead of $25,000, $24,000 instead of $40,000, or $45,000 instead of $60,000. All gross! You are obviously doing the work of more than one lawyer putting in those long hours. Worse yet, you are fooling yourself, and you're developing a work syndrome that cheats yourself and your family. By organizing your practice and time you can probably earn the same in the 40 hours and learn to enjoy other things than law. We have, and this work rule is inflexible except for real emergencies or when on trial. If you really try it, it will probably be self-perpetuating as you'll like the leisure enough to seriously fight for it.

The one month vacation. Here we don't mean four weeks, but one month. Again it's a discipline. Nor do we encourage splitting up the weeks as this is the first step to not taking it. We feel the lawyer is entitled to renew his energies and "charge his batteries." It makes no difference whether he travels or stays home since that's a personal decision. Almost invariably, our experience shows that with a one-month vacation he will spend all or most of the time with his wife *and* children. That is one reason for encouraging his taking it in one stretch and at a preplanned time, not just when he can "fit it in." If you're an older lawyer think back on how many times you've wished you could have spent more time with the kids, but it just never seemed to work out. As a younger lawyer in this age of more leisure why not make a habit of this welcome concept?

The month vacation can be taken at any time of the year. It can be before tourist season if there are no children's school vacations to worry about, or during a winter vacation. Its flexibility is a benefit, and we simply try to make sure more than one lawyer isn't gone at a time.

Parenthetically, we each attend one or two business conferences or conventions a year, which means additional time off from the office. As set forth in Chapter XVI, we encourage the wife to go along and here our experience demonstrates that the children are left at home. So if the event is 3 or 4 days, a full week leave is usual and while it's part work, it's also part relaxation.

Sabbaticals with pay. This perhaps is the frosting on the cake, the jewel of the diadem of a lawyer's labor. We are proud of its institution and continuance. Its one salient reason we feel we must practice with partners as detailed in Chapter V. When we first decided on it we talked of it for the future. Finally, my then only partner said "You're first, pick your year and go. If you miss, I go the next year anyway". We thus, happily started the plan. It's mandatory. It can be taken in one stretch or split in two parts. The lawyer can teach, study, write, do nothing, or as Marty says, "peel loquats," but he can't show up in the office. He's fully relieved of all duties or obligations otherwise imposed by the firm.

The Sabbatical leave is not a gift to the lawyer but an investment in his mental, spiritual and physical well-being. He will contribute longer and better to the firm, besides enjoying a longer span of life. We can't prove it, but we firmly believe that such a periodic pause in our vocation will result in less strokes, cardiac problems and hypertensions than our peers. Even if that weren't true, look at the unforgettable pleasures.

The planning is simple but rigid. We know several years in advance the order of rotation and whether it's a six month leave for the older partners or three month leave for the new partners. This allows spouses and children to plan also. We've each taken children out of school for extended trips and there's never been a problem that arose from it; to the contrary, the benefits are notable.

We've already regimented ourselves and our clients into

recognizing us as a *firm* and not a collection of individual attorneys. Having learned this tenet the problem was resolved, and it was then just a question of a plan to shift cases when the sabbatical came. This meant double teaming in certain matters was a hidden cost of the program which we bear, not the client, but it's well worth it.

Clearly, communications, staffing and, most importantly, mutual trust are required. An attorney may feel that his career may be jeopardized, his client relations tarnished, his days away from the office may be agony (they have never been yet). All these fears should be anticipated and openly discussed so that the attorney and the firm are enriched, rather than imperilled, by the sabbatical. Incidentally, it must be recognized that one of the risks of the program is that one of the attorneys may decide not to return. He may decide to continue to teach or to change his career or life style. So be it! We recognize that if that happens, the firm will survive and possibly be better for having a system that adapts to such change normally, rather than traumatically.

We believe that the above programs have increased our profitability in the long run. Not just dollar profitability, but the intangibles of physical and mental health also.

RULES:

1. Never work on Saturday, Sunday or nights except when on trial or in a real emergency.

2. Take one month vacation a year.

3. Take a Sabbatical vacation.

EPILOGUE

I've re-read the twenty chapters above after a short period. I'm convinced more than ever that our office is no exception and that any one lawyer's office or a firm of any size can Make More Money, if you're willing to slightly change your procedures. But you have to do it purposely, consciously and continuously.

I've suggested some basic (and perhaps novel) ideas here and THEY WORK. Don't laugh at them or, worse yet, ignore them.

If you will set up your office procedures in a sound business like manner and then incorporate the ideas set forth in this book you will be adopting the MMM principle. You will Make More Money for yourself.